RETREAT AND GROW RICH™

The entrepreneurs guide to profitable, powerful retreats

Darla LeDoux

Author Contact: Aligned Entreprenuers.com

Thomas Noble Books
Wilmington, DE
www.thomasnoblebooks.com
ISBN: 978-1-945586-02-6
Library of Congress Control Number: 2017934226
Printed in the United States of America
First Printing: 2017
Editing by Gwen Hoffnagle
Cover Design by Elie Colomeda

Dedication

This book is dedicated to family – biological and chosen.

Thank you for who I am becoming.

Contents

Introduction

I am a recovering engineer. I grew up believing that the way to get and keep love was to be smart, have it all together, solve everyone's problems, and never let my feelings show.

It worked well. I got good grades and was a top student. I got a degree as a chemical engineer and set my sights on working for one of the most competitive companies recruiting on the University of Minnesota campus, Procter & Gamble. Within two years at P&G I was promoted to senior engineer and my career was soaring.

As a smart girl I never once considered that I wasn't on the fast track to something important. I grew up in a town of 500 (502, but who's counting?). I would likely have become a doctor but I was in too much of a hurry to get the heck out of Dodge and start making money to invest that kind of time in my education. That, and blood scares me.

I fit well in the corporate world. While my colleagues would likely have described me as a bit unique – always asking the questions others didn't ask and looking to get to the *truth* of what was going on with our projects, our customers, our work culture, and more – I also knew how to toe the company line.

Having been raised in a household with alcoholism around several corners, I learned at an early age how to pay close attention to what people wanted and give it to them. Good mood? Be entertaining. Bad mood? Hide and keep quiet. Knowing what people wanted without their saying it… I was an expert. It got me gold stars… and a fast promotion.

But the intuition that helped me deliver was a double-edged sword. I could pick up on what made other people happy as easily as I could breathe, but I could also pick up on what our customers wanted, what they really needed, and what would happen next in ways that were highly inconvenient. I knew when a project was ultimately not going to work, when we were behind a trend, and when management had its head in the sand.

In the corporate world these sorts of opinions weren't exactly welcomed. At least not without data to support them. Because my opinions weren't generally valued when I was growing up, it wasn't a surprise when my opinions were dismissed. It was actually comforting.

In fact a career as an engineer was perfect for someone who wanted to prove she was smart but didn't want to risk having opinions that might be wrong. The data made our decisions. And while it was frustrating, and limiting, I also loved it.

I loved the prestige of my job title. I loved that there were rules, there was structure, there was protocol, there was data. My project either saved money or it didn't. Our product worked or it didn't. I found comfort in this place where I could feel safe. I could focus strictly on the external measures of success and avoid looking within.

Never mind that some of the specific career development advice I received early in my career went something like this: *All of that touchy-feely stuff that you like to do is great, Darla. We love your people skills. But just be careful not to spend too much time there. Your soft skills will only get you so far.* I knew it didn't feel right to buy in to that belief, but I assumed they knew better, so I went ahead and toned it down to fit in with the model of success I was given.

About five years into my corporate life everything changed. I was working a lot and striving for the next level after my promotion, only I didn't know what I was really striving for. I didn't want my boss's job, so I began to look around for what I *did* want. I didn't see it. The work I was so devoted to was ultimately to get people to buy more products I really didn't believe they needed. And as time went on I became more and more uncomfortable with stuffing my intuition and presenting the data that my supervisors wanted to see.

It was at about this time that I was introduced to coaching. My company nominated me and twenty-four others in my division to be trained as coaches. We were to become "Consulting Pairs," which was a very specific approach to diversity coaching that centered around understanding our own biases and perspectives.

This initial coaching training required me to look within in a way I never had before. It was messy, painful, and confronting. And I loved it. I knew immediately that this was the work that would change the world. I could see that what we needed more than another consumer product was the ability to get real with one another, to connect, to share, and to heal so that we could become whole as human beings and free to be fully ourselves and fully alive. I was just scratching the surface of what I would come to uncover within me that would eventually guide my work and my life, yet I knew it was important and I would never be the same.

Because you're reading this book, perhaps you had some version of this experience in your own life. Whether it was a coaching course, a yoga or meditation training, a personal growth seminar, a healing, a life-altering illness, a death in the family, a divorce, or simply a moment when you saw something you couldn't un-see, something woke you up to a new possibility. And perhaps you're wondering whether you're brilliant or crazy to be thinking about making a living spreading that possibility to others.

I had those exact thoughts. For almost ten years from the time of that training I daydreamed about becoming a coach. I knew it was my calling to pass on what I had discovered about what happens when we let go of how we thought we were *supposed to be* and become more of who we *truly are*. Yet most people thought I was crazy. And honestly, I did too. After all, I was a chemical engineer; how on earth would I give that up to become a life coach? What would people think of me? And how would I ever make money?

Throughout this book I will share with you exactly how I gave up my safe, prestigious career to create a life of freedom for myself, one that makes a big difference for others. As I write this I'm still learning and growing. That will never stop. I'm developing new skills for teaching others how to follow in my footsteps and do what I have done. I'm growing in my ability to lead my team. I'm navigating the growing pains of being a business owner after seven years in operation.

And I absolutely love my life. As I write this introduction I'm looking out the giant wall of windows in my home onto the Puget Sound. I responded to my desire to live on the water and I cannot get enough of this view. I've created a business in which I can work from absolutely anywhere. I am in a loving and growth-inspiring marriage that would never have been possible had I not followed my calling and grown into the person I am today. I travel regularly to places of my choosing as a business expense. When I want to stay home, I do.

I'm confident in my business's ability to earn whatever amount of money I'd like, which creates so much more freedom than I ever had in a job. My revenue has grown by an average of six figures each year through the exact approach contained in this book. The best part is that I'm doing exactly what I love to do and bringing forward a message steeped in love and truth and connection. I get to bring all parts of me to my work *and* my life, and I love it.

It was nearly ten years from the time I got my first intuitive nudging about my soul's purpose to the time I took concrete action toward creating my business. I was afraid of letting go of the safe and "smart" career path called "engineer." I was afraid of what people would think of me if I started giving voice to what I saw and felt. I was afraid to trust my intuition and creativity in a world that has increasingly valued logic and rationality and linear problem-solving over the more feminine ways of making decisions. I'd worked so hard to learn how to fit into the corporate culture that held such incredible allure for a girl from small-town Middle America whose parents didn't go to college. How on earth could I let all that go? Yet the longer I waited, the stronger the call got and the harder it became to stuff what I knew deep down to be true into the confines of a corporate cubicle.

I am tremendously grateful for my time in the corporate world. Each job experience was a critical steppingstone to who I am today. I also know that some of the value systems so many of us were raised with are broken. We can feel it. We can see it as we look around at the violence, depression, and illness happening around us every day. We've been stuffing our truths for too long. In our race to be more, do more, have more, many of us have lost our connection to our own intuition, our divine connection, our humanity. I know I had.

And when we lose connection to ourselves, we lose connection with one another. I believe the bulk of the pain we experience in society today starts with the pain of disconnection. Kurt Wright, in his book *Breaking the Rules*, said that "we can only trust that part of ourselves which we have revealed to another person and had *validated* instead of *violated*."

As technology continues to speed up our society, we've left no time for this kind of connection. In our race for productivity there is an increasing expectation of perfection. Be perfect moms, be evolved spouses, have the ideal fitness regime, by all means don't show weakness, and especially never ask for help.

And we are building all of this on top of fear that we won't be enough, and shame regarding the parts of ourselves that don't feel safe to share. Whether you are passionate about serving people in business or want to help them improve their health, their relationships, their creativity, their careers, their families, or their sex lives, it's so important to help your clients shift the underlying fear that is keeping them stuck; to help them know and love all of themselves and build from a solid foundation of self-love that will ultimately change every aspect of their lives.

Enter the power of retreats. In *Retreat and Grow Rich* I will show you how to turn your secret passion and inner knowledge into a lucrative business and a life of freedom. I'll teach you a business model that allows you to LEAD with your intuition and support your work with logic, rather than the other way around, as so many of our crumbling societal structures encourage you to do.

If you already have an established service-based business, as many of my clients do, you'll learn how to stop trading time for dollars and undervaluing your energy and knowledge, and instead create leverage through the power of group work.

I will also make a case for *transformation* as the foundation of the business of the future, rather than information. While I love learning new information as much as the next person, my life has never been markedly improved because I learned a new hot tip. In fact I spent almost ten years reading self-help books and staying stuck in the same line of thinking that had me trapped.

In this era most information is available at our fingertips online. Ingesting information without transforming the root of what has you stuck only makes you feel worse. I remember feeling frustrated because I knew so much, yet nothing had changed; I needed guidance to see what I couldn't see about the patterns that were keeping me stagnant.

I'll share more about the art of creating transformation, and what that even means, as we move through the book. If you know it's your purpose to help people wake up to their values of love, joy, purpose, play, connection, intimacy, peace, vibrancy, and more, you are absolutely living and waking up at the exact right time. Your work is needed. Individuals and companies are finally investing in the soft skills that can make you hard cash if you are willing to step up and do the work of transformation that happens NATURALLY and almost EFFORTLESSLY when you know how to guide it through the power of the small retreat.

I will walk you through the steps of creating a profitable, transformational, retreat-based business. With my model, regardless of the type of service you provide, you absolutely can create a multiple-six-figure business with a foundation of just a few retreats a year. If you follow along and complete the exercises as you go, at the end of the book you'll have the outline for the three core offerings for your Retreat and Grow Rich™ system. You'll understand the flow of cash and clients through your business as well as the foundational information about creating transformation at your RICH Retreat.

First I'll help you evaluate whether the Retreat and Grow Rich model is truly right for you. I'll then guide you through the linear yet non-linear process of reverse-engineering your offering so that you are building with the end in mind and creating maximum cash flow along the way.

We'll move through a series of teaching exercises that allow you to tap in to the foundation of who you are and what you are about in your business. (I call this "Owning It.") Entrepreneurs who have been in business for years have benefited from these exact exercises to help them tune in to their own alignment at a new level.

I'll address money and value and how to align your mindset with actually receiving money for the work you love most! Woot!

With these foundations under your belt, I'll walk you through the mapping of your content, how to decide what gets covered in each of your three programs, and specifically what to put into your RICH Retreat and why. I'll also teach you the HEART offer formula for monetizing your retreats and working with the best clients year after year.

Finally I'll share some of my best insights about how to lead the room at your retreat, and the top mistakes I see retreat leaders make time and time again.

My desire is that this book impacts you on two levels. As the engineer-turned-coach who is a healer at heart, I plan to address both the left and the right sides of your brain (your logical mind and your heart-mind). My wish for you is that the practical steps I provide, from marketing to pricing and more, give you enough specific structure that you feel confident in knowing that your retreat-based business can be the container in which your life's work grows.

My even bigger wish is that the stories and examples contained in these pages help you know that you are not alone. May you allow the words to land and heal your heart of any shame or doubt that you carry about your thoughts not matching the value system around you. May this newfound confidence be a springboard for garnering support for your mission and give voice to the truths that lie within.

Chapter 1

The Way of the Transformational Retreat Leader

I'm in the middle seat of a Mercedes Metris passenger van on a country road in Italy, eyes pressed to the window, but my mind is a million miles away.

I have my standard issue iPhone headset plugged into my ears and I am praying. Praying calmly to Spirit, Source, the Universe, God, to give me the right next direction. This isn't an unfamiliar quest, though this time I ask with peace and certainty, and this time it's not for me. It's for the five others in the van who have trusted me to create an experience for them that will change their lives.

Over the years I've prayed many times for clarity. I prayed even before I had any semblance of belief it would work. I've developed a different sort of faith since running a business. It's a deep faith in what's possible, and it's changed my life. Moving through life with an inner knowledge that all is unfolding for the greatest and highest good, and trusting myself to tune in to the right next step when I need it (rather than attempting to control eighteen steps ahead), have been the greatest gifts I could ever have imagined. My own process of growing a business and leading retreats was the catalyst for this transformation.

That passenger van was taking me and my small group of clients from Cinque Terre (the "five lands") in the Italian Riviera up to the town of Gavi in the Piedmont region. This was my first international retreat. We'd had two days at our first destination, hiking along the coast in a one-of-a-kind environment at Cinque Terre, each person tuning in and reflecting on where they were at that point in their entrepreneurial journey. We also had amazing food and wine, and even a cooking class!

Sitting in that van, I had no plan for what to do next. Which is why I was praying. Praying for guidance through the next steps in my retreats had become an everyday practice. But never before had I taken such a huge leap to run a high-end retreat, with travel excursions, education, and deep inner work.

When I left U.S. soil, I truly didn't know how it would unfold. I had a clear intention for the outcomes of my clients' experiences in terms of how it would leave them "being" in the world. I had a brainstormed list of potential ways I could get them there. But the unknowns of traveling abroad with a group that wasn't yet connected were too numerous to plan for. I knew the inspiration would come in this two-hour trip in the van. And it did.

Through my headset came the words of Dan Millman from his book called *The Laws of Spirit*. I'd posted to Facebook a week before for book recommendations on Universal Law, something I study regularly to keep me grounded in my journey. This book recommendation from my Facebook friend literally popped off the screen and I'd downloaded it immediately.

As I listened on that van ride, I heard Mr. Millman share concepts I'd learned before in a way that clicked for the particular group I was leading that week. I knew enough about what they were butting up against by this point that I could pick out the gems on how to guide their transformation. I was so excited as the pieces began to click together for me.

The following three days were a beautiful unfolding of insights guided by a single exercise I crafted as a result of Mr. Millman's words. Today each of those attendees is in a *very* different life than they were prior to the trip, and I had so much fun in the process.

This is often the experience of the retreat leader. We know what it is we want to convey. We have some ideas about how we will do it. We do our best to map it out, and we "hold space" for Spirit to aid in the process – the exact right book at the exact right time with the perfect people, for example. Yet we have to believe in our own guidance.

I share this because as you step into being the leader you are meant to be – the leader who is already there within you – hosting retreats, traveling the world, and getting paid will be your reality. And it doesn't have to be hard. You don't have to have it all figured out or even know how it's going to go. There are lots of guidelines and strategies you will learn in *Retreat and Grow Rich* about how to structure your retreat and what to prepare. You won't jump in cold without a plan when you start your journey. Yet the beauty and joy of the path of the transformational retreat leader lies in the deep inner freedom you create for yourself.

When you learn to hold space for transformation and lead from your intuition, which is your partnership with Spirit toward the greater good, magic transpires for you and your clients. And the world is a better place for it.

The Way of the Transformational Retreat Leader

In the first retreat I hosted there were sixteen attendees, and I had binders and worksheets and 182 PowerPoint slides – and it worked! The people in the room made tremendous shifts and I generated a level of revenue that surprised me. Yet these results didn't come from the 182 PowerPoint slides or the expensively printed and diligently assembled binders. The results came from who I was *being* as a leader in that room.

Over the years I've come to recognize that while certain teachings and experiences do require carefully crafted materials, the true transformation in the room happens when your attendees step away from their materials and their need to know what's happening next and into an energy that allows them to move into something new.

This is a very practical book. It will help you structure a very simple business that can bring in multiple six figures of revenue (even seven figures depending on the choices you make). It will help you determine the content to teach at your retreat, and more. Yet my reason for writing this book is spiritual. I don't have a religious affiliation or any agenda around having you think or believe something specific. In fact, quite the opposite. I want you to think and believe like *you*. The real you. I believe you were born with a purpose inside you and that it is your soul's journey in this lifetime to uncover it and live in alignment with it. In doing so you will feel free, fully alive, and fulfilled, and experience joy and peace on a day-to-day basis rather than the pain and struggle that is prevalent in our culture.

When you live and model this philosophy, the energy you bring to your retreats supports others in stepping into that transformation in a way that no head-based degree of information possibly can. The biggest reward in choosing this path comes in your own happy, fulfilled, and peaceful life, and as a bonus for owning your own transformation, others get to tap in to the fruits of your labor via your intimate RICH Retreat. And you get paid. It's a pretty amazing win-win.

There was a time in the past when the arts – the creative arts, the healing arts, etc. – were highly valued and revered. Over time, steeped in fear of scarcity, society began to value accumulation. We began to value logic and efficiency, as those were the qualities that allowed for faster production of stuff. And we began to teach people that their value was in doing rather than being or expressing or enjoying, so they would make great assembly-line workers.

Most recently we've valued the *knowledge worker* — the person who can think and create and progress forward. As we've become so efficient, the competitive edge now lies in an ability to think beyond the linear approach. Efficiency is no longer the main driver as individual human beings demand more. Yet our creativity (our connection to the divine) has been trained out of us. In the new era of our growth as human beings, being someone who can tune people back in to who they really are and what is really true is highly valuable. Not everyone sees it yet. So a part of your work here is to pave the way and own it.

The way of the transformational retreat leader feels risky, because in making the commitment to lead others to take ownership of their own lives, health, relationships, careers, money, and more, you are committing to doing your own work in the areas in which you lead. You'll live out loud with openness and commitment to owning your *truth* in a way that is rare on this planet. And you'll learn to let go of control and trust that Spirit, Source, the Universe, God, Intuition, Goddess, Divine Guidance (or whatever your favorite name is for these concepts) has your back.

If you aren't in this work to create more fulfillment for yourself through living and working in alignment with your purpose, the risk likely won't feel worth it. But if that inner sense of peace and contentment *is* a part of the draw, there is something you need to understand about transformation. I call it the "hidden commitment."

Hidden Commitments and Conscious Commitments

We always get what we are committed to. Always. I've come to understand and teach this core truth, as it is fundamental to the way of the transformational retreat leader. Coming to know this is half the journey and the entire key to your own fulfillment.

If we always get what we are committed to, why do we so often feel like we are not getting what we want in life? Because what we want and what we are committed to are not always in alignment. And that is the crux of a life unfulfilled.

Most of us, most of the time, until something happens to crack our shell or wake us up, operate under a set of commitments that are hidden from our view. I call these hidden commitments. Until they become conscious, hidden commitments run the show without our even knowing it. And that is why life doesn't look the way we think it should. It's why people sometimes try and try to create a certain type of success yet feel as if they are stuck on the same hamster wheel no matter what they do. It's why I knew for almost ten years that I wanted to be a coach and lead retreats, yet I continued to look for some other answer to what I was meant to do with my life.

In spite of my surface desire to find the work I would love, my hidden commitments of being smart and making others happy were running the show and making it impossible to follow my desire, and I couldn't even see them. Finally, through the process of attending a series of small retreats, I began to see and name the patterns that were keeping me from trusting my path, and to invent new commitments that served the path of my *truth*. Becoming a life coach certainly wouldn't make me look smart or make others happy; I had to create new conscious commitments that could take the place of the ones that had been the go-tos of my subconscious. I had to create a transformation.

What Is Transformation Anyway?

Merriam-Webster defines *transformation* as "a complete or major change in someone's or something's appearance, form, etc."

I'm guessing that since you picked up this book you've had your own experience of transformation in one way or another. There has been at least one area of your life that has undergone a complete or major change. Perhaps it's your health, your career, or an important relationship. If nothing is coming to mind, pause for a moment to think about it. What is the change you've personally undergone in your life that motivates you to share your work with others?

The definition of transformation I've cobbled together from my reading over the years is as follows: *Transformation is generating active, ongoing practices that shift a culture's experience of the basis of reality.*

The way you behave in the world is largely based on your personal experience of reality. The way you experience life tells you what is true, or defines your reality. If you want your reality to change, you have to transform the way you experience your basis of reality. You have to change the view or the lens through which you see your life. And as you do, you naturally take on new practices. Transformation is not about mantras or affirmations; it's about shifting the basis of your reality – your beliefs, agreements, filters – at the core. When your belief shifts, the basis of your reality shifts, and therefore your result shifts in alignment with your new belief.

From your basis of reality you create commitments that dictate how you operate. Before you transform a specific area of your life, your commitments are generally hidden from view. The majority of your hidden commitments were formed before the age of seven, when you did not yet have a conscious mind. Your conscious mind is the part of you that has awareness. Awareness gives you the ability to evaluate and accept or reject a set of beliefs or commitments. Before seven you simply can't do that.

When I was five and spent time with my dad, rarely did he pick me up when agreed, which left me questioning my value. When on a visit with him and his family, I gambled for quarters at the adult table and won repeatedly, and I can still see my dad leaning back in his chair, putting his arm around me, and declaring to the group, "Isn't she so smart?" In my never-ending pursuit to earn my dad's love, I became committed in that moment to always being smart.

As an adult I wasn't aware that I'd made that commitment as a kid, and in fact it hardly seemed like a choice at all; it simply *was*. This is why for nearly ten years I couldn't get myself to risk doing something that might not be, or might not appear to be, smart. For me it was TRUE that smart equaled love. There was no other option.

In his book *The Millions Within*, David Neagle describes it like this:

> *The subconscious mind works like the hard drive of a computer. From the moment of your conception it is constantly fed information. This input starts well before the development of the conscious mind. At this point there are NO filters at all. EVERY experience is recorded. The associations between an event and an outcome are dumped into the data record with equal weight and relationships between an event and a response get lumped together.*

The process of transformation is nothing more than the process of uncovering a hidden commitment for what it is and consciously choosing a new commitment to take its place. Helping a client transform involves guiding them in untangling the associations they invented as a child that helped them survive in life and in choosing a new, conscious commitment that serves who they truly would like to become.

And here's the great news: Doing and guiding this work is not complicated. Transformation can happen in an instant, even though shifting hidden commitments and creating conscious ones is a journey of a lifetime. I've gone from having to be smart to allowing myself to lead from the heart. I've loosened my fear of disappointing people and created a commitment to trusting Spirit to run the show. I've let go of feeling shameful about being a burden and learned to ask for what I want. I've even embraced the idea that making others uncomfortable is actually a gift. I've gone from needing a man to being okay with being happily married to a woman. These are a few highlights from my own journey, and I trust there is more to discover and become!

Love > Fear

Transformation is a journey from the head to the heart, from scarcity to abundance, from ego to truth, from fear to love. These are the shifts you make when you transform hidden commitments to conscious ones.

Hidden commitments come from	Conscious commitments come from
Fear	Love
Scarcity	Abundance
Ego	Truth/Non-judgment
Be smart and give them what they want	Follow my heart and honor what I want
External motivation	Internal motivation
Surviving	Thriving
Self-protection	Faith
Disconnection	Connection

The retreat in which I used the 182 PowerPoint slides was called The Sweet Spot Business Retreat. While those slides taught all types of practical information, the fundamental premise of the retreat was that in order to work in your sweet spot, or in alignment, you need to transform your way of being from hidden to conscious, or from fear to love. Decisions made from love create abundance and connection and help you thrive. Decisions made from fear create scarcity and disconnection and keep you in survival mode. These are two distinct energies, and your clients will have the pleasure to tap in to your energy if you choose to create from love.

When you are non-judgmental and act with love, faith, and abundance, you can connect with others in ways that are simply not possible when you are afraid. Fear breeds disconnection or separation. The source of the bulk of the world's problems today is the illusion of separation and the feeling of disconnection. We are more and more connected online, yet feel increasingly isolated. We are afraid of connection. We are afraid of intimacy.

My friend Kristi shared with me the idea that the word *intimacy* is parallel to the phrase "in-to-me-see." This idea resonates deeply. At the time of our conversation I'd been working with entrepreneurs for almost five years. I'd helped them understand themselves and market and brand their work in the world. I'd helped them transform hidden commitments and ensure that they would not return. But I was looking for a deeper way to express my work. I wanted to graduate from having people be and see themselves to guiding them to let themselves be seen.

I began to notice that nearly every hidden commitment my clients had adopted to survive their childhoods and make it out alive hid the real them from view. As a girl I took on "smart" rather than showing my heart, as my heart had been hurt too often to count; and letting my intuition be seen, as I had judged my intuition as wrong. My clients had taken on roles of fierce independence, having it all together, being the rescuer, being the perfectionist, being the pride of the family — and all these roles were mechanisms for hiding the REAL them. Somewhere along the way they'd decided the real them was bad, wrong, or otherwise not enough. As a result they were terrified to truly be seen.

And yet being seen was all they longed for. It's what we all long for. It is the great healer and equalizer. Being seen and known for who you truly are at your core has a transformative power that no level of knowledge and understanding can match. I've experienced it myself and watched countless clients take on, even physically, a whole new appearance as a result of simply becoming who they were. Wounds heal, hearts recover, confidence builds, and truth prevails. This is small-retreat power at its finest.

To lead such an experience you need not be perfect, have everything working in your own life, or have "arrived" yourself. You simply need to commit to stepping into your truth when it's vital and doing it transparently, quickly, and with grace and ease. (Kicking and screaming can work too… just keep stepping!)

The Decision Grid

Now that I've revealed that the first transformation in your new business will be your own, how are you feeling? In the exercise at the end of this chapter I ask you to make a clear decision as to whether or not you want to retreat and grow R.I.C.H. – whether or not you are willing to let out the **R**ight-brained, **I**ntuitive, **C**reative, and **H**eart-centered leader you are and trust that you will be valued in this currently left-brained world.

The "decision grid" is a tool you can use to consistently discern your *truth* and flush out any hidden commitments that could sway your situation. Remember, a hidden commitment is a belief or behavior that developed in response to something that happened in the past. Holding on to a hidden commitment makes you believe you will stay safe, as it has worked for you before, but it also keeps you from making decisions that will lead you to lasting fulfillment. Hidden commitments cause you to make decisions from fear. *Conscious commitments* stem from decisions made from love.

The decision grid helps you get clear about where your conscious commitments lie. First phrase your decision in the form of a yes-or-no question such as "Do I want to become a transformational retreat leader?" "Should I sponsor the event?" "Should we start a family?" or "Is it in my best interests to go to this party?" This grid works for any topic!

Then create a grid with four quadrants. The questions to ask yourself in order to fill in each quadrant of the grid are shown in the grid below.

	LOVE	FEAR
YES	1) What are the love-based reasons I would say yes?	2) What are the fear-based reasons I would say yes?
NO	3) What are the love-based reasons I would say no?	4) What are the fear-based reasons I would say no?

Now go through the quadrants in the order indicated above, filling in the *reasons* you would make the decision yes, and the *reasons* you would make the decision no. For every decision there are always love-based reasons and fear-based reasons. When it's hard to make a decision it's often because you can't discern the love-based reasons from the fear-based reasons. You default to fear-based reasons because it feels safer; it holds the illusion of safety.

It's ideal if you can do this with a coach or someone who is not personally involved in the decision and can help you dig beyond the surface reasons. The more skilled you are at accepting your *truth* the easier it is to do this alone.

Let's walk through a quick example. Let's say the question is "Do we start a family?" Here's how this could play out:

	LOVE	FEAR
YES	Excited to see how we might do at raising children. Want to be able to instill our values. Enjoy what it means to have a family – dinners together, school functions, etc.	What if we don't have kids and we're alone when we're old? The clock is ticking. We'll be left behind by our friends who have kids. Boredom.
NO	We love time alone together exploring the world. I can focus more on my business and making an impact.	What if we're not good at parenting? What if kids change our relationship and we don't know how to handle it? Kids will limit our travel and fun.

As you walk your way through the grid, you'll find that the bulk of the reasons are not new thoughts. They are likely thoughts you had before in a variety of ways as you considered your decision. There are probably one or two that hold a bit more emotion or trigger a gut response, letting you know that there is more than meets the eye. That's your entry point to your hidden commitment.

In the example above all the reasons are pretty standard, and they were not new to the client who went through this exercise, with one exception: "Boredom." This was listed as a fear-based reason to say yes to having kids, meaning there was a fear that without adding kids to the picture, they would get bored as a couple. This was a new awareness that showed up as a result of walking through this process. And because of the emotional response associated with the awareness, we knew it held within it a hidden commitment and that addressing this fear would be the key to a clear decision.

The hidden commitment was discerned as a commitment to "never being bored." Looking into that commitment revealed that being bored felt like a distinct possibility WITH or WITHOUT kids. When the client discovered why she had a commitment to avoiding boredom and made a choice to no longer let the fear of that run her life, she would then be free to make her clear and CONSCIOUS decision about whether she wanted kids rather than avoiding the decision because of fear.

EXERCISE:

Make a Decision — Is Being a Transformational Retreat Leader Right for You?

Your assignment for this chapter is to make a decision about whether being a transformational retreat leader is right for you. You can use the decision grid to help you to make a clear choice, using the blank one below. If you're anything like me, you probably want to move quickly to the next chapter without a clear decision. Perhaps you want more information. I get it. I encourage you to invest the time in tuning in to your thoughts about the decision, as finding any hidden commitment (fear) is likely to make reading the coming chapters more valuable. Your retreats will likely serve clients who are experiencing fears similar to the ones you've worked through, so the process is a true win-win!

	LOVE	FEAR
YES		
NO		

Congratulations on making your decision to lead transformational retreats! (If you decided NO then we part ways here… no hard feelings, as a clear decision is a gift and I honor it.) Meet me again in chapter 2 where I introduce the system that will be your engine for both cash and transformation for years to come!

Chapter 2

The Retreat and Grow Rich™ Business System

It's 4:00 a.m. and Kate is awake again. Today she is getting up an hour earlier in an attempt to get all her work done. Two nights ago she was *still* awake at 4:00 a.m. finishing her work. She heard a knock on the wall from her husband beckoning her to come to bed, but had to ignore it. She loves being an entrepreneur – at least the IDEA of it. She knows she's here for a reason. Yet this business thing is not all it's cracked up to be. She went into business to create freedom and joy and to make a difference, and now she feels like she's falling short on all fronts.

Sound familiar? That was less than a year ago. Kate was making enough money to get by, but not enough to thrive, and certainly not enough to make all the long hours worth it. A former stage manager, capable of fulfilling on all manner of heroic acts, she was also certified as an online business manager. In that role she supported other business owners in getting things done. Whatever was on their plates went onto her plate, in addition to managing her own business offerings, and the work load was never predictable.

She'd even offered to help some clients hire the rest of their team members, as she happened to have a gift for hiring. She would write job descriptions, post the roles, conduct screening interviews, and set up appointments for the prospective hires to meet with the business owners. All for one low flat rate.

She knew she wanted to create more freedom for herself, so she decided to create an automated virtual course. As many people do, she started asking entrepreneurs what their problems were as research for developing the course. Before she knew it she had created a plan. She would develop a program to help people manage their email. This seemed to be the biggest problem people consistently had – being stuck in email hell. She had a system she used for herself that she could teach people!

Now she was delivering all sorts of services – hiring people, marketing her new online course... no wonder Kate was overwhelmed! On top of all this, to be a "good" business owner who did all the "right" things, she was attending events, networking, studying online courses to stay up to date, booking speaking gigs (or feeling bad about not doing it), attempting to write a newsletter, and on and on.

She was still frustrated because she knew there was something more inside her that she was meant to give. Even though her weighty workload affected every area of her life, she had visions of hosting dinner parties and spending long hours painting. But she was doing none of those things.

Thankfully one of the courses Kate took was my Retreat and Grow Rich virtual program. It quickly became apparent that she was doing most of her tasks for one of three reasons that are so common among entrepreneurs (and you're not alone if you've been doing them for one of these reasons!):

1) It was what she believed people would pay for
2) It was what other people told her to offer
3) People needed it and she was good at it

Kate learned that this outside-in method is not the way to make business decisions! Instead she needed to work inside-out. She needed to look at what was important to her, what difference she wanted to make in the world, and what she believed was the best way to help create this transformation.

She also needed to look at what she wanted to be doing on a day-to-day and month-to-month basis. She needed to know what she wanted her life to look like, including the lifestyle she desired and the money needed to support that lifestyle. Where did she want to travel? Where did she want to live? How did she want to spend her work time – programming emails in her clients' customer relationship management (CRM) systems, or out in the world connecting with people and leading retreats that made a difference? She had to look at what her true genius was and release the rest.

Releasing familiar things can be challenging because you might have built your whole identity around what others told you to be or do. You might be very good at things that are not your genius, but your genius will always make your heart sing, make time fly, and create an effortless momentum. It isn't hard or stressful, and it doesn't bring up resistance within you.

Kate discovered that her genius was actually not in the things she was getting paid for. Though she could do them well, they were bogging her down, making her procrastinate, dragging her hours out, and creating a very unhappy and exhausted Kate. She discovered that her genius was in the things her clients were getting from her *for free!*

In addition to her stated services, Kate was providing her clients with all kinds of coaching. She could see what was working for their businesses and what wasn't. She intuitively knew what was causing them strain. And it was safe for them to tell her the truth about their business frustrations. She helped them process thoughts and ideas that they weren't sharing with anyone else. She was really making a holistic difference for them. Given a better way to deliver this genius of hers, she could truly serve clients and find greater personal satisfaction in doing so.

I'm going to talk a lot about "containers" in this book. I like to think of your business offerings as "containers of support." I learned this term from Michelle Conboy, one of my first coaches, and it really stuck. A container has sides and a bottom that represent the boundaries or constructs that you set up for your work with your clients. When you put something fluid into a container, it spreads out and fills that container, getting into all the corners without even trying. Yet it can't creep outside the container; it stays focused.

When you create a container for the support you offer your clients – the definition, intention, and boundaries of your offerings – they can more easily buy in to the nature of your work. When you and your client come to an agreement about the container, the work becomes focused and efficient. This is the magic of the Universe and the power of co-creation and intention.

Kate's work needed a different container. Her clients, and loads of other people, would benefit from her coaching genius unencumbered by all the busywork she was doing. She wanted to work with clients who really wanted to get honest with themselves – clients who wanted to be powerful in how they were running their businesses so they could make their dreams into realities right now rather than putting them on the back burner. She needed to design a container of support (a retreat) for her clients to do that type of work with her so that the *real* Kate could absolutely shine!

And shine she did. She first had to release the bulk of her clients, but those who stayed with her moved into a whole new way of working with her. We spent a short time mapping out her signature Unleash Your Dreams retreat, which required much less content than you might think.

She filled her first retreat by calling people she already knew who needed that type of transformation. She hosted two retreats in a row, filled her first High-Level Program (more on this in chapter 7), and suddenly had her very first period of sustainable income. Kate and I began our work in April. The year prior she'd made £43,000, the equivalent of ~$60K in U.S. dollars. By focusing on her genius and doing the work she loved, she booked more than £40K in sales the first month. She crossed six figures in six months, and today is on track for a multiple-six-figure year.

With that momentum and certainty, Kate continues to break through the barriers that were blocking her from having a simple business and a wildly fun life, learning how to create the money she wanted and deliver her work in a way that was simple and fun. Today her 4:00 a.m. wake-ups are by design, as she prioritizes meditation and her spiritual connection.

Everything shifted when Kate stopped making choices that reflected the hidden commitment of putting herself through the "emotional wringer," as she called it. As she stepped into her own power, she realized she was in a relationship that no longer served her. And in fact, part of the reason she'd kept so busy was that she didn't want to have the free time to face that she and her spouse wanted different things. She began to travel and do things that fed her soul. She did all the things she'd wanted to do and expected to do — from experiences that freed her physically and emotionally to indulging in an art retreat, and more. The more she followed her inner compass, the easier it became to make money. She booked retreats in places she wanted to go, and as she traveled, attended events, and met people, she invited them to her upcoming retreats. She learned that her gut could be her guide, and that she was allowed to have fun and make money. She stepped into a life of freedom.

As she made the transition, Kate regularly sent me emails from her clients sharing their successes and thanking her for the difference she had made. They were some of the most powerful acknowledgments and breakthrough stories I have ever read.

Using the Retreat and Grow Rich Business System, not only did Kate create the freedom she craved as an entrepreneur, but she was making a difference in the exact arena that mattered to her most!

Here's the great news: You can be like Kate. Your story may not be the same — your genius is unique to you, and the life you want may be different — but you have a unique genius, and there is a way to package this gift such that you love your work and have a huge impact on your lucky clients!

When you strategically design your business so that you offer your best work to the world and let go of the rest, you're able to charge more, your clients receive better value, and you have a lot more fun!

For most service-based entrepreneurs on a mission, it's easy to get caught up in starting in the wrong place. Some offer everything they can think of to anyone who will buy it, thinking more clients is always better. The problem with this is exactly what we've seen with Kate — you are busy not only delivering the work but also managing your mind as you shift back and forth between different types of projects. And there is a limit to what you are able to charge when you don't focus your expertise. A generalist can't charge as much as a specialist.

Others are busy building an online marketing machine, what my friend Angelique calls "The Willy Wonka Machine." They build complicated marketing funnels without first getting real-life experience with the right clients from which to develop their online marketing.

I love online marketing because it allowed me to create a business I could move with. I was able to move from Cincinnati, Ohio, to Denver, Colorado, in my third year of business with zero negative impact on my results because my clients could now find me online. But it didn't start that way. I spent a long time building the *wrong* stuff online. In trying to model what I saw other people doing, I spent a couple of months launching a mastermind program online. It was called Decide Then Thrive, and while the principles I planned to teach were solid, my marketing was terrible, and no one purchased. The marketing didn't work because I talked about what I believed people needed and should want rather than what they actually said they needed and wanted. Since I had developed almost zero online audience, I was saying the wrong things *and* there was no one there to read it anyway! Unfortunately this is not uncommon.

I'm a fan of an approach that allows you to get real-life experience with your ideal clients as quickly as possible *and* establish a consistent cash flow in the process. I call this the LEARN approach, which I discuss in chapter 8. Whether you are brand new in business or want to transition your business model into one that leverages your time a bit more and brings in more money with fewer clients, the Retreat and Grow Rich Business System is likely to bring you tremendous freedom.

The Retreat and Grow Rich Business System

Are you ready? I'm excited to introduce you to the Retreat and Grow Rich Business System!

For years I was a big advocate for uniquely customized businesses. In fact I often talked about the idea that following someone else's formula for success doesn't work. I do still believe this, and in fact it was a challenge to begin teaching a specific approach. (I still don't like to call it a formula.)

So please use my approach as a springboard and customize it to work for you. I always tell my clients to learn the formula, then break it. You can spend years of your business life trying different ways to package and offer your services, spinning in indecision. I've seen many people do this. And while they may learn a lot, and I am not here to judge that path, I know that the sooner you choose a business model that feels right for you, the sooner you will create your freedom.

Choices lead to freedom. If you choose your approach and stick to it, you free up your time to create highly effective marketing and to be creative and innovative with your programs. Your energy is much better spent there than in trying to decide what to do first and second and third. I encourage you to trust yourself and make the choice so you can move into the fun stuff that really matters: meeting the right clients and bringing all of yourself to the way you serve them!

There are four main stages to Retreat and Grow Rich (RAGR):

1) Own It.
2) Offer It.
3) Amplify It.
4) Elevate It.

The Own It and Offer It stages are foundational and they don't need to take a lot of time, but are key to knowing yourself and understanding what you want to create. This is where you do the initial work that Kate did, declaring your unique genius and the difference you want to make, and beginning to *be* that in your market. This is an inner journey that creates the confidence you need on the outside to draw the right clients into your programs. You "Own It" in terms of your place in your market. Then you "Offer It!"

The Offer It stage is where you learn to take money for the work that comes easily and naturally to you. This is foundational work because without it you will continue to give your genius away or work harder than you need to. In this stage you get used to bringing in money, get your initial systems in place, and connect with your first new clients and ask them to pay you. You'll learn loads from actual human beings whom you talk with!

Stage three is Amplify It. To amplify is to expand, make larger or greater, increase the strength of. In stage three you expand or increase the strength of your work in the world through the development of three strategically designed programs that allow you to market and serve most efficiently for the biggest impact. The three offerings you'll develop in your business are:

1) Your Gateway Program (Gateway)
2) Your RICH Retreat (RR)
3) Your High-Level Program (HLP)

The three offerings together create a system that gracefully prescreens for ideal clients so that ultimately you work with the exact perfect people (I call them STAR clients) in your High-Level Program. Your Gateway Program is a client's introduction to you. It is priced to reach more people, and lets them decide if they want to dive deeper. The RICH Retreat is where they can integrate and deepen what they've learned in the Gateway, and transform what would otherwise get in the way of their getting a result. The High-Level Program is designed to get the best result in the most efficient way. It won't be for everyone, but for the right people it's perfect. The elements of the system all work together so you can create powerful marketing that brings those right people in from the start. We will cover each of the offerings one at a time throughout this book.

The fourth stage is the Elevate It stage. You'll know it's time to move into the Elevate It stage when you've mastered the flow of clients through your three offerings in the Amplify It stage. You will have developed systems that make delivering these programs easy and simple, such as using technology to automate steps and a team to support some of the delivery. When delivering your programs feels simple, and your cash flow is solid, you'll have the time, space, and energy to innovate. This might be creating an additional retreat offering, writing a book, offering "done for you" services, or even certifying other people to do what you do.

This book focuses on the first three stages, as it takes time to reach the Elevate It stage, and once you get there you will know what to do!

The Client Journey

I like to think of the flow of your clients through your system as a journey with you. You will reverse-engineer your programs, developing them from the highest level to the lowest so that you design everything with the end in mind. But before you do that, I want you to have a clear sense of what it is your clients will experience.

For years I taught this using the analogy of a bus ride, so we'll start there. Imagine all of the potential clients in the world, and they are lined up at a bus stop. Now I know you are imagining WAY too many people, because you still think that you want to help everybody, but that's okay.

Each of the people lined up at the bus stop is in a certain type of pain. They may or may not be aware of it, but if you think about it, we all have pain. Whether it is a physical discomfort, an emotional pain, or the pain of wishing something was different in our lives, we all have something. I'd love to lose some weight right now, for example.

Each of these people also has a certain set of desires; there is some experience they want that they don't yet have. We are designed to desire growth and expansion.

So each person at the bus stop wants to get out of the pain they are in, get to the destination they desire, or some combination of the two. You will design your RAGR business system to help them do just that. But not *all* of them – a certain highly specific subset of them. (We'll uncover who your STAR clients are in chapter 4.)

You are the bus driver, and you're taking a group of these people, your STAR clients, on a bus ride from the pain they are in to the destination they desire.

You can think of your marketing as the marquis on your bus, the sign that lets them know as quickly and clearly as possible where you are taking them so they can make a clear decision about whether they want to get on your bus. Keep in mind that your bus has only so many seats, so you don't actually want all of them to board the bus. And besides, there are certainly some people you do not want to take a road trip with, right?

There is likely some distance between where your STAR clients are (the pain at the bus stop) and where they want to be (the benefits at the destination). They are not going to go the distance overnight. And in fact, they may not even be sure that they are ready to go the distance. Some may think, feel, and believe that they are, yet in truth they don't quite know what it means to go the distance. Because rarely can we see the entirety of a journey when we're at the starting point.

That's why you break down your bus ride – your client journey – into smaller offerings, each one moving them closer to the destination and helping them decide if they want to go all the way.

Imagine that your bus takes clients from New York to Los Angeles. Some people know right away that they want to go straight to the destination. Others are not so certain. So you offer them a quick trip around Times Square before they make the decision to leave the city with you. (This is the free education you give away in your marketing.) Some people might choose to take part of the journey with you, to Cincinnati, for example, and perhaps that's all they need, or they decide your bus isn't for them and they catch someone else's the rest of the way. This is *totally* okay, because your STAR clients will go all the way.

To stick with the analogy, you can think of your three offerings as selling three different tickets en route to L.A. Sure, they can buy the direct fare, but most will choose one segment at a time. Your Gateway Program (Gateway) will get them from New York to Cincinnati. Your RICH Retreat (RR) will get them from Cincinnati to Denver, for example, and your High-Level Program (HLP) will take them all the way to the specific address they are looking for in L.A.

Your client engages with you first through your marketing, which is primarily free. They then invest in your Gateway and take the first steps toward achieving their goal. Next they attend your RR where they INTEGRATE the information they've learned in your Gateway and move further along the route. After they've experienced working with you in the RR, your STAR clients will want to stay with you for the long haul as they change their lives to align with their goals.

What's so great about this is that at each step your client is choosing the next step because they get you and they get where you're going together.

One of the biggest challenges that entrepreneurs face, especially those who are in the world of transformation, is "explaining" to potential clients what they do and the value of their work together. When you have your RAGR system in place, by the time you ask them to invest at the high level they don't need an explanation because they get it and they know you're their person. The best part is that because they get it, when you kick off together in this way it makes them much more fun and easy clients to work with!

Reverse-Engineering Your Client Journey

Hopefully the flow of clients through your programs is making sense and feels exciting. Now you're probably thinking, "What goes in my programs and how do I market them?"

That's the perfect question, and I have to tell you, I don't know! But that's what you're going to sort out as we work our way together through the chapters ahead. Before you can pick what goes in your RR and decide how to structure your Gateway, you must understand the big picture of how *you*, uniquely, get people from the pain at the bus stop to the enjoying the benefits at the destination. You must understand what happens on the entire journey and know the ins and outs of the outcomes your STAR clients get in your HLP. Then and only then can you define the entire path!

Many transformational workers want to host retreats, and they think, *What would be fun to do? What do I feel like talking about?* Yet they haven't strategically mapped out a journey that will move their clients to the big-picture outcome. Reverse-engineering your client journey is the pathway to creating money and lasting client impact.

The Flow of Clients through Your Programs

Just to give you something exciting to look forward to before we dive into who you actually are in the world, I want to give you a quick rundown on the numbers. Many of my clients have goals of working with roughly twelve people at any given time in their HLPs. I've found it to be consistently true that roughly half of the attendees in an intimate retreat go on to participate in a higher-level offering. This means you'd need to host twenty-four people on retreat to bring in twelve new clients. I recommend doing this in two separate retreats of twelve.

In my experience anywhere from 50 to 75 percent of those who join a Gateway will attend a retreat to integrate what they've learned and work with you in person. Let's make the assumption that your results are on the low side, and half of your Gateway participants come to your retreat. This means you need to have forty-eight clients in your Gateway to hit your goal of twelve in your HLP.

Let's say your main marketing strategy is speaking. When speaking, a good goal to shoot for is that 20 percent of the people you speak to will purchase your Gateway (which can be super simple, by the way). Twenty percent is one in five. This means that for forty-eight people to purchase your Gateway, you'd need to speak in front of 48 times 5, or 240 people to hit twelve in your HLP. You could do ten groups of twenty-four or two groups of 120, or anywhere in between!

If you price all three of your programs appropriately (you'll price them in later chapters), you can actually develop your multiple-six-figure business from that one group of twelve clients. This means that over the course of a year you only have to speak ten times to groups of twenty-four, or once to 240!

Just to be clear, you might not hit all your numbers on your first time out of the gate, but in short order you truly can simplify your business and create more space in your life!

The RAGR system is for the entrepreneur who wants to spend more time *being* and less time *doing*. If that sounds like you, then read on.

The Top Four Myths That Keep Entrepreneurs from Diving into Their First Retreat

Myth #1: I have to have a big list before I can host my first retreat or event.

Having an email list is great. There are some people who claim that as long as you have an email list you have a business. I haven't seen this to be necessarily true. I've met business owners who focused diligently on list-building for long periods of time, yet never learned how to monetize their lists. Bringing in *clients* and *cash* requires three stages of marketing: meeting, engaging, and activating. It's easy to meet people, and relatively easy to engage them if you are willing to share generously. Activating them to take action to work you with you is a whole other skill set that you will develop through hosting your retreat. You don't want to wait too long to learn to do this or you will have a big list and no money.

The truth is that you can fill a retreat without a list. You can meet, engage, and activate someone to attend your retreat all at once in a networking meeting, through a speaking gig, or by sitting next to them on an airplane (this happens all the time for some of my clients!). When you are clear about the transformation you deliver in your retreat, you are naturally activating.

Myth #2: I have to host a big event to make big money.
One of the strategies I implemented when I was in my "do everything people tell me to do" phase of business was to host a big event. All of the most successful entrepreneurs I was spending time with were doing them and there was this idea we all held that if we could just have a big annual gathering, it meant we had made it. We'd make most of the money we needed for the year and could relax. We'd be super popular, too, because lots of people would know us as word spread about our amazing event!

You can hear in my language that many of us were hosting events for the wrong reasons. I did make money from my event. In fact I booked multiple six figures from clients in one of them. But I have repeatedly made just as much PROFIT from an intimate retreat with about 5 percent of the effort.

My bigger events cost me almost six figures in expenses. They also consumed six to eight months of my time in planning, marketing, and filling them. And while being on stage is always fun for me, the whole *process* of the event was not.

A small retreat creates more intimacy than a big event. You know the participants and you know who your best clients are. They get to know you intimately and connect in a way that makes them want to continue working with you beyond the scope of the retreat. You'll have fewer people buying your programs just because you're a celebrity, which means your clients will tend to stick, and stay with you for years.

Myth #3: I need a lot of speaking experience to host a retreat.

The biggest question I get from people in regard to hosting a retreat is "What will I say for two-and-a-half days?" They are concerned they won't have enough content or don't have enough speaking experience.

Guess what. Hosting your own small retreat is one of the best ways to *get* speaking experience! You will learn in chapter 6 that you need much less content than you might think to fill the time. But the best part is that it's actually much easier to speak in front of your own audience than it is to win over someone else's audience. Hosting a retreat is a great way to practice speaking. You can test out different concepts and exercises on a very forgiving audience, then turn those into your signature speech!

Myth #4: People won't pay for my retreat.

I will teach pricing in more detail throughout *Retreat and Grow Rich*, but the crux of my approach to retreats is to offer an initial retreat at a relatively low price, and from that point offer the right people a chance to work with you at a higher level. That said, I have hosted and attended high-end, topic-specific retreats offered for very high investments (five figures for five days, for example). When you understand your audience and own what you deliver, it's a perfectly wise investment for your clients!

Is RAGR Right for You?

The RAGR approach is right for someone who is, or longs to be, a bit more right-brained. It allows you to think non-linearly and trust your own connections. It's right for the entrepreneur who is, or wants to be, more intuitive in how they operate their life and their business. It's not important that you consider yourself "an intuitive," as that label can scare off a lot of normal folks who shut down their intuition early on (as I did – it took me years to reestablish this connection).

You are a RAGR person if you seem to "just know" things. Maybe you just know what to say when someone comes to you with a problem, or perhaps you just know, feel, or intuit trends happening in your marketplace or in the world. Your intuition helps you discern *truth*, which is of huge value to people who attend your retreats.

It can be necessary to move through a process of your own transformation in order to reclaim your sense of intuition. I know I'm not alone in recognizing as an adult that much of my intuition was diminished in my childhood. I've worked with many adults who were able to reclaim a prior intuitive ability. As a child, when the adults you love behave as if something is perfectly normal yet you can pick up on undertones about what is really happening, you doubt yourself and make the adults right. In my household we did a lot to tiptoe around an alcoholic personality. Some of the ways people behaved made no sense to me, yet I eventually gave up my inner knowing until, as an adult, I could put that strange behavior into perspective. I believe the process of reclaiming *truth*, one entrepreneurial leader at a time, is what will raise the consciousness on our planet and change the experience of being human.

The RAGR approach is for you if you long to be more connected in your work. If you've followed the formulas for how to create business success and found yourself unhappily checking your heart at the door, you'll be pleased that RAGR allows you to create deep fulfillment and awakens your self-expression.

The RAGR approach also works if you want to create a heart-centered business. You want to make heart-to-heart connections with your clients, have conversations that really matter, and unleash all the love you have for life and for people that too often gets buried deep down in our world of proving and striving and hustling. You know this new heart-centered path is the way of the future and you want to lead in that direction.

On a practical level, RAGR is for you if:

- You've been offering strategy sessions (discovery sessions, complimentary consultations) to fill your private work or high-end programs, but are running into price resistance. You know you are reaching people who can really benefit from working with you, but they aren't quite seeing the value. They want to say yes, but they aren't really sure what they will get. If you've had this experience more often than you'd like, RAGR will help you design an approach that allows your clients to know why they want to work with you without your having to fit all your brilliance into an elevator pitch or a short conversation. They get to know, like, and trust you, and are ready to invest at a higher level than they would based on a phone conversation.

- You deliver one-on-one work with your clients and you've been successful with that, but you're not leveraging your time. You are so busy delivering this work that you don't have time to market. Trying to work *on* your business and *in* your business is wearing you out. You find yourself saying the same things to multiple clients, and you know you could reach more people and save time if you shared your knowledge in groups. You want to develop a system that brings in groups of clients without having to work so hard.

- You are in a business that sells INFORMATION – maybe you market online programs or you teach people how to do something, but you want to graduate to selling TRANSFORMATION. You are ready to come out from behind the safety of all that you know and start offering people new possibilities for how they can *be* in life. You've started to recognize that even when people have access to all your perfectly organized information, they don't change; they don't use the information in the way you envisioned because you're not helping them integrate it. You want to risk speaking the truth in a new way because you've started to recognize what Tony Robbins has been saying for years – "information that is not attached to emotion is not retained," and you're ready for your clients to be more successful. This is only done through integrating your information into a live experience.

If any of the above sounds like you, and you have a heart for making an impact, and you know you want to make money doing so, then RAGR and the process in this book will help you know exactly how to do this.

EXERCISE:

How Easy Can You Make It?

The Retreat and Grow Rich Business System can make your life incredibly simple. I've consistently filled my retreats for the last year without actually doing anything to fill them. However, for the several years prior, while I was consistently filling my High-Level Program from my small retreats, I also wanted to do everything else I learned about! I had major bright-shiny-object syndrome.

If you can embrace the discipline to have just three offerings, and trust that with that system you are serving your right people in the right way, simplicity awaits.

In this exercise I want you to imagine for a moment that you have all three of your offerings developed. You have one (possibly two) core marketing strategies, your Gateway Program has been automated, and you simply show up to lead a retreat two or three times a year and you have a room full of STAR clients who want to work with you further. Your community has a life of its own!

What is the immediate thought that comes up? Is it "Yeah, right, that's not possible" or "Bring on the simplicity!"? This exercise is a simple way to ground you in the *truth* that it can be easy.

Make a "T" chart on a piece of paper, drawing a line down the middle to cut it in half, and making a space for two headers.

On the left side write the header "Why I might make it hard" and on the right side, "The benefits of making it easy."

For example, on the left side, common reasons people make it hard include "I got messages from my parents that hard work equals success" and "I wouldn't know what to do with myself if I weren't busy working on my business."

The right side can include some of your personal goals that are important to you in your free time, like "Time to write my book" and "Time to connect with my family." A big motivator for many of my clients is their own integrity; that is, "Because that's what I teach."

Extra Bonus Exercise: Whatever your reasons are in the right-hand column, ask yourself how you can have more of that right now... before you even begin!

Why I might make it hard	The benefits of making it easy

Great job! I hope you've decided to make it easy! In the next chapter we'll begin to focus on finding alignment within yourself about what your retreats and your business are actually about. Let's Own It!

Chapter 3

Own It, Part I – Your Clarity

When I give a talk I often share a photo of myself taken when I first started my business. I say, "I was no different from you. I had no advantages, no special superpowers." In the photo I'm wearing a standard black suit, purchased at Express, with a "pop of color" in my top underneath. I'm wearing big black glasses, and my hair is swept sweetly to one side (which still happens from time to time). I look like I'm about twelve years old. A nerdy, sweet, twelve-year-old engineer who left the safety of her corporate bubble to pursue a business most people told her (to her face *and* behind her back) would be a disaster.

Luckily I still look a bit young for my age. And luckily those people were wrong. But not without valid concern. While I understood product development, and I understood marketing, and I had done a stint as a ninth grade teacher, I had no experience selling myself. I knew how to use data and had great instincts about how to allocate seven- and eight-figure marketing budgets, but I had no idea how to go about selling a service that existed only in my imagination. I knew on some deep, heart level that what I could bring to the table had value, yet the idea of actually receiving money for it and trusting that my service would make a difference... well that was paralyzing. I constantly distracted myself with busywork so I wouldn't have to face taking the action that would ultimately result in my asking for money.

There's a bright side to this story. I did, in fact, go out into the world and sell myself. I did, in fact, grow my business through all the fear, terror, and insecurity. There is one reason I did this, and one reason only. I knew my "why," my reason for being in business, and that made it worth moving through the fear and having people actually notice me. That's what this chapter is about. My goal is to help you find your reason, too.

But first let me bring my initial terror to life for you.

I pull up to the Buca Di Beppo Italian restaurant in Hyde Park, Cincinnati. I'm driving my 2000-something black Toyota Solara. This car isn't exactly "on brand" for me. I bought it from my old roommate for some kind of a "great deal" after I sold my Buick LeSabre to my shady neighbor for cash. The details of both transactions are firmly forgotten. I'd gotten the Buick from my mother after my stepdad died, because she really wanted an SUV now that she didn't have him to drive her around the snowy streets of northern Minnesota. I share this because downgrading my vehicle was one of the ways I had made my life small after my divorce, preparing to start my business. My finances were not strong as a result of marrying someone who had addictions. And I was 100 percent certain that following my passion and doing the work I loved was going to mean eking out a living; I'd prepared myself for that.

I'd signed up for a business networking group I found at Meetup.com called "Positive Connections," and the first meeting was taking place at Buca Di Beppo. I'd never been to a business networking group before in my life. I'd grown up in the sheltered world of corporate life where someone above you told you when you needed to go to training, and you went. Or someone above you taught you to always be on the lookout for good training, industry events, and other boondoggles that the company could send you to – preferably in an exotic location. In other words, I'd always attended company-sanctioned training and events with other colleagues where the content was structured and the expectations were clear. Attending a meet-up felt like the Wild West. What would happen? Who would be there? What was the point of all this? Would I stack up? (That last one being the *real* question.)

I did what any CEO of a burgeoning business would do. I went to the bathroom. And then I left.

Yup, I walked into the restaurant, caught sight of all the confident entrepreneurs laughing, exchanging business cards, and sporting their best business suits, and immediately retreated to the ladies' room. I stood in the stall of the Buca Di Beppo bathroom, with the paintings of the old-world Italian women smiling down at me, and I panicked. My inner dialogue was in stereo. The mean girl was shouting at me about how stupid I would be if I drove all the way here and didn't go in, and how was I ever going to do this business if I couldn't shake one person's hand. The kinder, gentler part of me, who knew she was here to help people love and trust themselves and stop being so mean, was advocating for a loving approach to myself, which at that moment involved slinking out the door. I was terrified to trust the "loving" approach; how loving would it be to just let myself off the hook like that? I'd love myself broke! Yet who was I going to *be* walking into that room carrying the mean girl's nasty dialogue in my head? I was so damn conflicted.

Have you ever had a moment like that when you feared doing the thing and also feared *not* doing the thing? And you're not sure which side is winning? Suddenly you're caught in a whirlwind of questioning yourself. You can envision both choices, but you worry that you're going to be wrong either way. One inner voice tells you that if you don't push through and do the thing right now you will never succeed and you'll be homeless. The other side chimes in to remind you that if you do the thing from a bad energy of pushing, it won't work anyway, so what's the point?

If that sounds all too familiar, you're not alone. When you are an intuitive entrepreneur who follows your heart, it can be easy to get confused about where your heart lies and where your fear is blocking your knowing: *Is it my heart, is it my intuition, or is it my fear?*

In that moment, at Buca Di Beppo, I made the decision to leave. In hindsight, I know that the better thing would have been to go to the meeting, honor the commitment, and be loving to myself by letting go of whatever pressure I had put on myself to do the meeting "right." I could have just had fun, enjoyed, and observed so that I could learn. I now know that whenever I am in doubt, I should follow through. We can't get more information about where we actually *are* in doing something without following through to get a result. We often think we can predict how the experience will go, but we can't. It's critical that we get used to taking action, even if it means doing the action "badly."

That said, I forgave myself for not attending.

I've shared this story many times, and I know people relate to my sense of insecurity and fear about doing a thing "wrong." But what I have never shared is that prior to walking into the restaurant I had just had a phone conversation with my brother. He'd conveniently called me just at the time I was heading to my event, and he was not doing well. From the time my stepdad had died, inspiring me to pursue my dream, my brother had gone the other direction. He had turned to drugs and alcohol to numb his pain. And when we spoke he was clearly intoxicated and talking about how he didn't want to live.

My brother was born when I was fifteen years old, and this was the first time I'd ever had a conversation like that with him – a conversation that involved real emotions like depression and death. My relationship with him has clearly been a part of my soul's journey, and it's surprisingly intimately linked with my business journey as well. As of this writing my brother has overdosed several times, and is still alive and still working on his journey of sobriety.

When my brother told me he didn't want to live, I was deeply shaken. I remember thinking, *Oh my God, he wants to die, and I have to do something*. My emotional state was the perfect excuse to give in to my fear and leave the event without entering.

When we are afraid, any small thing can stop us from following our dreams – a phone call, a stomachache, a scheduling conflict, a traffic jam, a questioning family member, a sideways look… and I was no different.

I was also no different when it came to how I managed my business. I am a social person. I am an extrovert (though retreats are *definitely* not just for extroverts!). I love to create with other people. I knew that one of my biggest challenges in running my own business was going to be working alone. I'd worked on teams for most of my career. As a teacher I was actually pretty isolated because all the teachers were so busy with their own work that we rarely socialized, and that had been tough for me. So I knew I needed to work with people from time to time. I did what I have seen lots of people do when starting their businesses, before they know better: I took advice from the wrong people. In my desperation not to be alone, I set up a regular, formal structure for meeting with my former corporate colleagues.

After a couple of months of struggling on my own in the dark, each day trying to figure out what I should do first and how to market myself, I quickly became lonely and isolated. I started binging on chocolate-peanut-butter-chip ice cream and obsessively working on my spreadsheet of how much money I was going to make once my business was up and running. I knew I needed to reach out to someone. I had loads of smart friends from my prior jobs whom I loved and who had great experience in the realm of marketing and product development, and I decided to ask for their help.

What was great about this action was that I actually asked for help! This is a key skill for an entrepreneur to learn, because if you can't ask for help you'll never ask for money. (Informal study by Darla LeDoux ☺)

What was not so great about it was that I was trying to market my heart by committee. Once a month we'd come together, I'd serve dinner and wine, and I'd spend a bit of time educating them about what I was up to, what I'd learned in coaching school, and how I envisioned teaching it. They'd ask me some questions, then I'd present them with my dilemma, which mostly centered around how the heck to market my coaching, and they would brainstorm ideas for products and packages that they thought would sell.

At the end of one meeting the committee decided it would be a good idea to offer workshops for moms to help them get their "sexy" back. Woah, what? I wasn't a mom, and I wasn't worried about getting my sexy back. My friends were generating great business ideas that had nothing to do with the journey I envisioned and everything to do with their *own* journeys.

The fundamental flaw of my approach was that I was asking this committee to tell me what was in my heart, and it doesn't work that way. Not to mention that no one on my committee had ever run a successful business, and most of them were very tied to the security of their own corporate jobs. It wasn't the right environment for cultivating what was in my heart. At the end of most meetings I felt *worse* than I had going in.

It wasn't the committee's fault. What was in my heart to do was given specifically to me. And what is in your heart to do has been given specifically to you.

I'm actually a huge believer in using community to create what you want in your life, and that is actually the premise of RAGR and why I love that you're considering creating a transformational retreat. I don't believe you can find your truths alone. But you can't ask your community to search your heart for you. They can only be mirrors for you to see your own truth. And you want to select the right mirrors – people who are already there or are going where you want to go.

Even with the right community, you still need to own your own vision. You need to own what you believe and what you want to create, deep down in your heart. That is your secret weapon.

Even with the level of fear that caused me to skip my first networking event, and even with the level of uncertainty that had me create an elaborate committee structure to market myself, I still got traction and I still grew a business from ground zero. I was able to do this because under all the fear I knew what I believed, which was that who you are being is more important that what you are doing, and that if people can learn to focus the power of who they are being (their energy), they will experience the freedom to be fully themselves and find the joy and peace that go with that.

I didn't get into business on a whim. I didn't do it because I thought it would be easier than a job, because I didn't want a job, or because I wanted to make money. I did it because I wanted to help people live more joyful, peaceful lives. This mattered to me, and that was all I really needed.

I see so many entrepreneurs spend so much time behind their laptops trying to come up with clever marketing slogans and designing elaborate offerings that never see the light of day, and it breaks my heart, because I did all of that. I tried to think my way to being successful without allowing space for any failure, and that didn't work. I'm sure you've heard this idea before, but it's so damn true: the more willing you are to fail, the more likely you are to succeed.

Before my stepdad died and I failed at marriage, I was pretty stuck on making sure I was successful, or at least looking like I was successful. Even as I started my business, I really wanted to do it "right" – I could have spent my life waiting to get it "right" before I moved forward. If I had done this, I wouldn't have millions of dollars in revenue under my belt and be sharing my journey with you. But my "why" in business – my reason for moving forward with what was in my heart to do – was greater than my fear of failing. It's the single biggest reason I'm still in business today.

When I finally did make it to networking events, I would stand up and share my elevator pitch. Many times I sat down and the negative thoughts roared and screamed inside my head, *What did I just say? I should have said X instead. Did I make any sense at all?* But inevitably at the end of the meeting someone would come up to me and say, "I'm not sure why but I think I need to work with you."

Have you ever had this experience? It wasn't my perfectly crafted pitch – I said something different almost every time. It wasn't my beautiful website – they had never seen it. It wasn't my client testimonials or years of proven experience – I was new to being a business owner. It was my OWNING my belief about the work I do, and being in alignment with it, that made all the difference. In our busy and oversaturated world of information, this is rare, and therefore valuable.

OWNING IT is an energetic thing, not a formulaic thing. It's something people *feel* from you that surpasses all logic. You can't own it and stick to someone else's formula. Owning it has to do with believing what you say and saying what you believe.

I love this quote from Larry Winget, who is known as the "Pitbull of Personal Development" and was a mentor of mine for a season: "People will never listen to what you have to say or believe what you have to say, but they will always listen for whether you believe what you have to say." I find this to be so true. This is the power of alignment. This is the power of owning it.

So what do *you* believe? What do you know to be true, deep down in your heart, based on your own experience and intuition? Why did you go into business in the first place?

I'm certain you understand, or at least understood at some point, the truth about why you do what you do. This truth is the way you view the world, which is so unique to you that your STAR clients will gladly pay you for it.

It's not unusual to completely forget the reason you went into business, especially if you open yourself up to marketing by committee and follow the committee's advice, tips, and tricks for marketing your business. But don't worry, your why is still in there! It might be buried under all the Google searches you've done and your observations of other entrepreneurs, but it's uncoverable. And I'd love to help you uncover it now.

I'm going to walk you through a thought process for discovering what I call your Clarity Point™, and I'll share some tools for getting to brand clarity. Just as you don't want to market by committee, *there is no need to fit yourself into these specific tools.* But my clients are often blown away by how these tools help uncover their clarity. I receive all sorts of comments about how they help the pieces click into place so they can "Own It!" Yet I always want you to take what works for you and leave the rest. If you can embrace the essence of this process, it will work for you even if you don't like the full template.

Let's do this!

Your Story

I hosted a training recently in which people had lots of opportunities to ask me questions. They asked me how to find the right people for their retreats and what kinds of experiences they should be offering. These are questions that I can't answer outright without digging a bit deeper and learning more about them. How can I know what you should offer without really knowing you – your heart, your background, your perspective, your why?

Simon Sinek, popular leadership consultant and author, has a terrific book, *Start With Why,* in which he goes into great detail about the successes of companies that are really clear about their why. Companies that are clear about the reasons they do what they do and the differences they are committed to bringing forth in the world through commerce are more successful than those that are fuzzy about their missions. The differences are remarkable. When a company has its why at the forefront, it is in it for the long haul. It always has that touch point to come back to when making decisions. Without that strong, clear rudder, it's easy to go astray.

One of the stories that stood out in *Start With Why* is the story of Samuel Pierpont Langley. He went to work on inventing a flying machine at right about the same time that the Wright brothers did. Langley had many more advantages – more money, more people helping him, etc. But Langley's why had to do with becoming famous. He wanted to be the first in flight to look good and smart and be admired. (I can relate to that!)

The Wright brothers, on the other hand, had a vision of how the world would change if we could fly. They had a grassroots team of friends and colleagues who supported them, and they enrolled each of them in fulfilling their bigger vision for what was possible.

Langley set out to fly and didn't get off the ground. The stories of his failure traveled around the world. Because his motivation came from his ego, his shame at this failure was so great that he quit. The Wright brothers also failed, and then they tried again. Because their commitment was from the heart, they were willing to risk failure, accept it as it came, and move on toward their goal with the knowledge and new understandings their failure brought them. And the rest is history.

That's the short version of the story, and there are two lessons: One, when you come from the heart in the work you do, when you have a reason to do it that matters to you, you won't quit because of a temporary setback. My first business mentor used to say, "Businesses don't fail; business owners quit," and I believe that. They quit because they aren't committed enough to live through a temporary failure to find the lesson and the eventual success. Two, when you can tell the story of your why in such a way that people are left thinking, "Well of course you do this work; you were meant for it," any questions about credibility go away, and people can see and feel the real you, ready to be of service. Just like the Wright brothers had a tribe of committed supporters, you will also create a tribe of committed clients who work with you for reasons that go beyond money or time. They want to be a part of something bigger than themselves. They feel good about choosing you over other providers because they align with your values and they want to see your bigger mission succeed.

In answering questions related to what someone should offer, I ask for a bit about the person's story in relation to the work they do: "Why did you get into this type of business?" "In what way have you experienced what your clients are experiencing?" "What was the turning point in your life that caused you to make a similar change?" "In what ways are you like your clients, or is there someone in your life who is like your clients?"

Tapping in to your story is incredibly important in uncovering your why. When you dive into your story (in my live retreats we do a meditation to tune in to key life moments and turning points and map out the story on a giant timeline), you gain an understanding of the experiences that shaped you and made you the perfect person to bring your business to life. And with the right view of the puzzle pieces, your purpose and value become abundantly clear.

Your Unique Perception

I'd been working with clients to laser-in on their missions and purposes for a little over a year when I read a book called *The Intelligent Entrepreneur* by Bill Murphy. In it Murphy said, "Your business should solve the problem that you are uniquely positioned to perceive in the world."

When I read this, bells of recognition went off. *YES! That is it! That is exactly what I've been helping clients discover. Their unique perceptions.* And I started using this language to help clients realize that they are the only ones who can do their work in their way. You are the only one who can do your work in your way. Because no one else can see what you see. Period.

Think about some of the moments you experienced that felt like no big deal, certainly nothing worth writing about, yet they cemented a thought, a knowing, or an idea that went on to shape your life. Yes, stop right now and think about those moments in your life… they are integrated into your way of being in the world that makes you powerful beyond having simply learned something in a book or having gotten a degree or certification. In fact, plenty of people have degrees and certifications for things they stink at. Your unique perception is something entirely different.

It isn't one thing; it's a combination of moments in your life that taught you what is important to you. It's what you naturally tend to notice or see in the world. This perception can come from where you grew up, places you've lived, jobs you've had, or even quotes you've heard that really spoke to your heart.

I'll share some examples from my own life that made me passionate about helping people be free to be themselves in business. I grew up in a small town where everybody knew everybody else. I observed that small-town living could be lovely, but it could also be cruel. Because everybody knew everybody and there wasn't a lot to do, most people where harsh judges of other people's actions. So and so is lazy, and such and such is a homewrecker, and on it goes. I have since learned there is gossip in all circles; however, it is especially rampant in a small town. For me this created a lot of fear of ever doing anything wrong. I watched this communal judgment destroy lives and put people in boxes. I got a firsthand view of the power of judgment to create disconnection and isolation. Small-town life even inspired me to work with my fellow high school students to develop self-esteem training that we delivered to the fifth grade class, creating awareness that they were awesome no matter what anyone else might say about them!

I was a female engineer. At that time, as a woman, I was firmly in the minority. I worked in packing development, a highly male-dominated engineering subset. While there is no big story here, the fact that I was out on the factory floor at age twenty-four telling groups of manly men how run my line test is a part of who I am. I learned some things about how women and men work differently, even though at the time I wasn't necessarily looking for such lessons. That knowledge is now part of who I am and what I bring to the table.

When I was training to be a coach while working my corporate job, I spent fourteen days in a training program with a group of employees from all levels in the food and beverage research and development department. We were required to be vulnerable and honest, and any lack of truth was noticed and called out. I saw firsthand that the vice presidents were no different from the administrative assistants when it came to living in alignment with their truths or lying to themselves. I saw that those who run Fortune 20 companies are no different from you and me. This is knowledge that I now have in my bones.

Many of you are aware that most people are going through life faking it somehow and pretending to have it all together rather than trusting their authentic selves. Because I had that training, and have seen this truth show up in people across a broad spectrum of education and income levels, I know it's true. So when I meet people at networking events, for example, I know that even if on the surface they seem put together, it's highly likely that there are some deficits in authenticity and connection to self.

When working with people who are creating their own businesses, I am super confident that I can help them see that they can do it – because I know they have as much or more going for them as the people running big companies all around the world. I also know, because I watched myself and my colleagues evolve from our training, that the more real and authentic a person is, the more ease and joy they can create in their life!

Some of my favorite quotes that shaped how I live my life are also part of my perception and knowing. "Life isn't about finding yourself. Life is about creating yourself," from George Bernard Shaw, graced my giant chalkboard wall for a year. Martha Graham, the revolutionary choreographer influenced me with *"There is a vitality, a life force, a quickening, that is translated through you into action. And because there is only one of you in all of time, this expression is unique. And if you block it, it will never exist through any other medium and will be lost."* And there is Maya Angelou: *"A woman in harmony with her spirit is like a river flowing. She goes where she will without pretense, and arrives at her destination prepared to be herself and only herself."*

These are just a few illustrations from my life that reveal how my experiences add up to the way I view the world. Studying the trends in my failures and successes in business has added to my unique perception as well. This unique way in which I view the world is a big part of what people are buying when they hire me privately or attend my retreats.

What is it about the way you view the world that makes you unique? What have you seen or experienced that gives you a distinct advantage as a service provider for a particular person? What quotes have moved or influenced you? When someone decides to work with you, what perceptions are they buying? Where do you come from in your work? Your unique perception is a huge part of what people tap in to when they work with you, both practically and energetically. For most services we purchase, we want to work with someone who sees something we don't see. This is how we grow.

The more you can own your unique perception, the better. As information has become abundant on the Internet, people are buying less and less of what you *know* and more and more of what you *believe.* The savvy client is aware that the most valuable training they can buy is in how to think and how to be. Through being fully aware of how you think, you can own what you're selling beyond your time and information. In the small-retreat format you won't have to tell people about how you think; they will see it as you lead the room.

A health coach who grew up with a sick parent and was continually exposed to the impact of poor health choices has a different perspective on wellness than one who was a high school athlete and went on to become a bodybuilder. A business coach who lost it all in a prior business and then rebuilt something more sustainable has a different perspective than a young entrepreneur set on working as little as possible and traveling the world. Can you see how none of these perspectives are good, bad, right, or wrong? They simply embrace different perceptions and attract different audiences. Knowing where you're coming from makes all the difference in knowing who you truly want to work with.

Your Clarity Point™

Here is where your story and your unique perception come together as your Clarity Point. Knowing your Clarity Point helps you walk through life with a certain confidence regardless of what is going on for you. Your Clarity Point helps you define your brand, but it is not a tagline or a public statement about what you do. In fact, you might not ever share it with anyone. But it can still be your guide! It is just for you! Isn't it cool that you get to have something that is just for you in your business?

Your Clarity Point is, as Oprah likes to say, "What you know for sure." When you walk through the world, you naturally observe or see or believe things about people and life that make a difference. For example, I once dated a guy who from a young age would get physically upset when he saw other people litter. He couldn't help but notice it. And imagine this: he went into environmental work! Your Clarity Point provides a filter through which you interact, helping you determine who needs you most.

Your Clarity Point is not focused on your specific business. You can apply it anywhere in your life. This is great because there is so much freedom in discerning what you are about regardless of what you do to earn a living. For example, I didn't know I had a Clarity Point when I started my business, but I did. And it is the only reason I was successful, because everything else in me wanted to stop and hide in the bathroom. Here is what I knew for sure:

Who you are being is more important that what you are doing.

This small statement is singlehandedly responsible for my business success. Discovering that what I call "beingness," or the energy we embody, is what creates our results and matters more than what we actually do, was life-changing for me. That knowing, because I had experienced it, allowed me to hold a deep conviction and confidence about who I could serve. When I shifted my energy, or way of being, in regard to the debt I had when I left my marriage, a series of seemingly miraculous events occurred that resolved the debt in no time. I had done experiments, such as when I was a teacher I taught a certain lesson to a group of students employing one kind of energy, then intentionally shifted to a different kind of energy when I taught the same lesson to a different group of students, and I experienced an entirely different result. I knew an energy shift would change outcomes, and I saw when someone would benefit from a shift in their energy.

You can shift who you're being in a situation, and the entire situation changes. For example, if you're being resistant to a certain marketing strategy, even if you do the strategy exactly perfectly as taught to you, the energy of resistance creates an unfavorable result. However, if you are being excited and confident about the strategy, results reflect this. I've often seen people shift their energy about something, and the thing changed. And I really wanted other people to experience this too, because I knew we didn't need to be working so damn hard. We didn't need to keep doing more to create results; we could do less and actually be more aligned with what we wanted to create. Whether you agree with my Clarity Point or not won't change what you get from this book; it's just something I know for sure.

My Clarity Point was super helpful because in the beginning I didn't know exactly how to do business, and I certainly didn't know enough about what other entrepreneurs were dealing with to be able to solve their problems. But I did know I could read their energy and pick up on who they were being, and I knew I could walk them through a process to help them transform ways of being that weren't serving them. I believed that would make a big difference in their lives. (I eventually discovered that I wanted to focus on helping people be aligned with their truth in business, but in the beginning I didn't know this!)

Whenever I felt overwhelmed or doubtful or feared I was not enough, which happened often, I remembered this knowing. When I walked into a room full of entrepreneurs, I used this knowing to help me pick out my STAR clients. They were awesome people who were doing a lot, but I could tell by their energy they probably weren't getting the results they desired. They were focused on doing, and unaware of the being part of the equation. Because I knew I could help them, I easily (well, mostly easily) approached them to talk about how they hoped to transform their business.

When you discern your Clarity Point, it changes everything about how you relate to yourself and your business. For example, when Rhonda arrived at one of my retreats, she had identified four potential target audiences for her work as a professional coach. She was passionate about a lot of things, and had many different sets of skills and experiences and different types of training in her toolkit. She was an M.D. and licensed in several alternative health-care modalities. It was easy to see how she could create just about anything. And in fact various people had given her different advice about what she should do. She was overwhelmed.

By looking at the chronological timeline of pivotal moments in her life and digging deep into her unique perception of the world, she was able to put the pieces together and discern her Clarity Point:

Connection is healing and healing is connection.

Based on this clarity Rhonda quickly reviewed the four options for who she could serve and chose the one that was most aligned with this idea. Who would most benefit from understanding that power of connection to heal themselves physically, and also spiritually? She began bringing her Clarity Point forward in her role of managing weight-loss clinics with her family, and was able to create more fun and energy in that role for herself.

As I've grown into my business my Clarity Point has evolved. And as I write this book I can see it may be in the midst of evolving again. As we collect experiences, we see things differently. As we act in ways that expand our comfort zones and put us into new scenarios, our energy is drawn to new ideas, and new visions download.

For the past few years, as I discovered trends in why entrepreneurs stop themselves short of full-on success, and as I walked on my path of exploring connection and intimacy, what I began to see loud and clear is that most people avoid intimacy (in-to-me-see). Success is challenging because most entrepreneurs employ complicated strategies to avoid being truly seen. The deep fear that they are not enough makes them hide.

My new Clarity Point became:

You have to let yourself be seen.

As with any good Clarity Point, this allowed me to spot my clients in a room. They were awesome, of course, but whether by looking like they had it all together or by showing up smaller than they really were, they were keeping the world from seeing the real them. With my new vision, I viewed them clearly.

What is your Clarity Point? What is that one statement that is a declaration of what you know for sure will make a difference to your STAR clients? Another way to think of it is if your clients could take away one thing from their work with you, a single belief or understanding, what would that be? Here are some guidelines for figuring out your Clarity Point:

- You are certain about it – it is an absolute *truth* for you.
- It is easy to remember, not something you have to look up.
- It helps you to discern STAR clients. Just the thought of it brings to mind the problem you solve and helps you recognize that problem in others.
- It applies to your business but is not your business; it also applies to other areas of life.
- It is for you and also for your clients.
- If your clients get nothing else from you but to embody your Clarity Point, you would feel as if you'd done your job.
- It is phrased as a declaration or a call to arms for people to agree with you. (Or disagree, which is also okay.)
- It moves you emotionally and makes it all worthwhile.

Uncovering your Clarity Point can be challenging work, as we often resist boiling down all that we are and know into a statement. However, having this level of focused clarity is what makes for a powerful business and life. There are, of course, additional factors that go into building a business and a brand. I teach a course called Your Brand Pulse, which starts with discerning your Clarity Point and builds from there, defining your points of view, your three core promises, your articulated benefits, and your brand's values and attributes. We won't get that deep in this book. If you are just starting your retreat business, you will discover a lot of this as you host your retreats. Knowing your Clarity Point is more than enough to draw in your right crowd!

EXERCISE:

Discover Your Clarity Point

1) Take out a clean sheet of paper. At the top of the page answer the following question, writing the first answer that comes to mind without overthinking it.

**If I could get everyone in the world to
agree with me about one thing, what would it be?**

2) Read your answer. Now write your response to the next question on your sheet of paper.

What would that make available?

In other words, if everyone agreed about that, what would now be possible for them? Or phrased another way... "So that what?"

3) Now continue to ask the question "What would that make available?" until you fill the page (possibly a couple of pages) with responses. For example:

*I would want everyone in the world to agree with me
that who they are is enough.*

What would that make available?

They would feel good about themselves.

What would that make available?

They would not be judgmental or upset with others.

What would that make available?

They would actually feel supported by other people in the world.

What would that make available?

They would be able to be more generous.

Etc.

4) Review your list of statements or declarations. Which grabs your heart? Which is the crux of the matter? Which statement is the one you can stand by, that you know for sure, and that makes all the other statements true? (It is possible that it's a combination of two or more of the statements. For instance, in the above example I might combine the last and first to say "Generosity creates abundance.") Circle your statement of highest resonance. This is your Clarity Point.

There might be more than one statement that feels absolutely true to you. If this is the case, it's okay to have more than one for right now. Put each of them on Post-it notes in your office and live with them for a week. It's highly likely you will be able to discern "the one" as you live with them. Remember not to overthink it! The power is in your belief that you are doing it right!

Great job! You've considered your story and the perspective that makes you unique, and chosen a Clarity Point that can guide you in the next step of choosing your STAR clients based on who needs you and your Clarity Point most! That is the work of our next chapter. See you there!

Chapter 4

Own It, Part II – Your Client

Alexis was so awesome. You know those people you meet who are just incredible? She was one of those people. (All my clients are those people actually.) There was a depth to her that revealed a lot going on under the surface, and what she said and created came from the deeper wisdom within her. I'm guessing that because you're reading this book, you're actually one of those people, too.

When I met Alexis she was doing "okay" in her freelance graphic design business. She'd established her client base over the years and received ad-hoc projects, from developing new logos and brand identities to reformatting brochures. There was a wide range for the price of her work. On average she was charging about $40 per hour. Some projects she did for free because they were fast and easy and she figured that person would hire her later when they had a bigger project; it seemed more trouble than it was worth to bill for such small things. Thankfully she had a spouse who had a good full-time job; otherwise it would have been pretty unmanageable.

Some of the projects she truly loved. Some of them not so much. The same with her clients. She had some who lit her up and some who were big pains in the ass. She wanted to explore how to do things differently.

As I began to work with her, I started right in with her personal story. Why was it that she was in this line of work, and what did she truly care about? On the surface she felt that she came to it by default. Art was the thing she was good at, and she found refuge in creative classes in school. She happened into a design job through a connection and never looked back.

But as we explored further there was more to the story! The reason she'd gravitated toward art classes was that she was dyslexic. She had trouble learning in the traditional way in school, especially in classes that required communicating with the written word. She found refuge in communicating visually, and loved that in design she could communicate without a word.

As we dove into that, we looked at what problems that experience and perspective made her uniquely positioned to perceive in the world. Who else had trouble communicating? How could her deep compassion for that issue help her position herself as ten times more valuable than anyone else who did the same thing? What client needed her most?

Based on her somewhat limited experience of promoting herself as a small business owner (she worked mostly through referrals), Alexis had noticed that other small business owners seemed to have a hard time talking about what they did. They would stand up and share an elevator pitch that didn't always make perfect sense. Not to mention that they would hand her the world's most confusing business card! The design did nothing to help the reader know the type of business they were in. It made her crazy! Yet she also had compassion for people who were having trouble communicating because she knew exactly what that felt like.

As she started to pay attention she realized that these heart-centered entrepreneurs had trouble communicating in other ways as well. They especially had trouble communicating with their designer what it was they wanted their design to look like! It was not uncommon for someone who made a living communicating in words to describe the design they wanted like this: "I don't know exactly what I mean but I think it needs to be more swirly." Or "I need it to feel more exciting." Or "I just want to smile when I look at it." Or the one she hated most: "I'll just know it when I see it."

As frustrating as this was for her, she had an advantage, which was that she knew exactly what it was like to feel frustrated when she didn't know how to convey what she meant. And because of this she was infinitely patient with clients who didn't know how to describe the design they were looking for. She could work with whatever garbled set of words they gave her and create a design that reflected the essence right back to them. And that was valuable.

Thinking through what made her so unique, which centered on her biggest struggle, Alexis was able to embrace the idea that her uniqueness mattered and was extremely valuable to the right person. She developed her tagline to include the idea of what a client's brand communicates, and she developed specific offerings that solved her STAR client's most pressing problem, specifically creating websites and business cards that expressed who they were without their having to say a word.

The best part is that this specificity helped her go from taking clients via referral only, at a range of prices averaging $40 per hour, to working with a specific type of client with a specific outcome and charging $8,000+ per branding package. Overnight. No more degrees or certifications needed. No time building up to the new rate. She had all the experience already; she just needed to position herself so her STAR client could see her.

While it sounds simple and straightforward, this wasn't easy for Alexis to embrace. What had shamed her for so long was now her "story" for her business, and she needed to put it front and center. The thing that was so easy and natural for her – her compassion and her ability to express visually – was now super valuable. How could she share this? Why would anyone care? Yet people did care.

Prospective clients care about where you come from and why you do what you do. They *want* to pay you for the thing that comes most easily and naturally to you. Because it's easy is exactly why they want to pay you – because it's *not* easy for them.

It's surprising that we struggle so much with this idea. If you think about it, this idea of uniqueness makes perfect sense. Certain things come easily to each of us. If we all did what comes easily to us and allowed others to do what comes easily to them, it would all be covered and we'd all have easy jobs. It's so simple. Yet we spend years of our childhoods learning that we need to work harder to be better at the things we're *not* good at in order to be a "good person" who gets good grades, etc. We create jobs that require us to work harder to be better at things we're not good at. F*ck that! Choose to work with the people who want what is easy for you, period. And enjoy the journey!

The STAR Client

Who is this STAR client anyway? STAR is an acronym. When I left my corporate gig I was hoping I'd left acronyms behind forever… but they actually work. Your STAR client is your ideal client. Your STAR client is a specific subset of what is often referred to as your *target audience*. S.T.A.R. stands for:

S – Smart
T – Tenacious
A – Aligned
R – Ready

Your STAR client is the client for whom you want to design all your programs to satisfy. The more specific you are about who this person is, the easier your programs are to market. I know how tempting it can be to want to serve everyone. I also know that many business owners get the concept of choosing a specific STAR client, yet somehow believe *their* business is different. But *specific* is really always better. In this chapter I share why choosing a STAR client – right down to knowing the thoughts that run through their head and where and how they shop for groceries – helps make you more money without getting any smarter, just like Alexis.

S – Smart. This may sound strange, but you want smart clients. I didn't consciously choose this client trait at first because I personally had my own baggage about the word *smart*. I was always known as someone who was smart in the traditional sense – I got good grades in school, I was a chemical engineer, etc. It was part of my identity. It was also what made me feel separate, sometimes judged, but more often than not simply trapped by some expectation of how I was supposed to be. I liked school and I liked that I did well, yet I couldn't help but envy the kids who didn't seem to care about their grades. They seemed to be on to something. They seemed to intuitively get that the whole grading thing was an arbitrary measure of something that didn't matter in the real world. (I probably gave them too much credit, but deep down I knew the game I was playing was invented.)

You want smart clients. I don't mean to sound elitist, but you want to work with clients you admire and respect and who challenge you to grow. The best part about your work is that you get paid to learn, so enjoy it! Too many people think that the really smart and amazing people would never hire them, so they don't set any standards for their clients. But it's not true. See yourself as worthy of damn smart clients.

Here's where my truth about *smart* comes in. Smart is relative. You get to define what smart means to you. We're not talking about someone who has a high GPA or the best score on a standardized test. What does the client who is super smart in your world look like? Perhaps they're smart enough to be open to Eastern medicine. Maybe they're savvy when it comes to techie stuff. (This would not be me, by the way.) Maybe they're super resourceful, and once they're clear about what they're doing and why, they do whatever it takes to find out how to achieve their goals. Or perhaps they're smart enough to know that their intuition will never guide them astray, even if they aren't always sure how to follow it. What does a smart client look like *to you?*

T – Tenacious. If your work involves client transformation, you want a tenacious client. Merriam-Webster defines *tenacious* as "not easily stopped or pulled apart; very determined to do something." You want a client who is determined in their intention for their work with you and will persist in hitting their goals.

Transformational work is not for the faint of heart. If someone is going to face and permanently shift their thoughts, feelings, beliefs, actions, and results at a core level, they will encounter resistance. Something will happen to make them doubt their commitment. (I call this the "Cycle of Proving.") Something will happen to make them feel that their goal is impossible. They will be afraid or intimidated by the truth they uncover or what they need to change to step up to a new level. It's bound to happen.

A tenacious client faces this truth and keeps moving. They call upon their inner resources and do what it takes to make the shift even when the challenge feels greater than they're up to. When you're defining your STAR client, what are the things about them, perhaps indicators from their past, that let you know they will follow through and do what it takes? What are the key indicators of tenacity?

A – Aligned. Your STAR client is aligned with where you want to take them. Of course you want to believe that everyone wants to go where you want to take them, but that's just not the reality. For example, of course everyone *should* want self-love, but some people aren't ready to love themselves. Some think that's hogwash. They are what I like to refer to as "not your people."

One of the most difficult things to learn is how to discern which clients are not aligned with you, and to let them go. It can be tough emotionally to meet prospective clients who disagree with you. It can be tough when you know you could really help someone in a hundred ways, yet their fundamental belief system or area of interest is not aligned with yours. You need to let them go. There are plenty of people who are aligned, love your value system, and want to go right where you want to take them. There is no lack.

Bless and release the unaligned and move on. For example, if you believe in past lives and it is a key piece of the work you do, you want to check this out with your clients to confirm that they can get on board with it. In my initial strategy session I often ask a prospective client to tell me about their spiritual beliefs. When the shit hits the fan, as it inevitably will, I want to know that they won't despair over it or blame me for it — that they will recognize it as Spirit guiding them to a solution.

One of the goals of my work at Aligned Entrepreneurs is to help people design jobs that never require them to suppress any parts of themselves; where they can be 100 percent transparent about who they are and what they are about and trust that they will be valued. If someone's not aligned with all of that, they are truly not my people.

My wife and I recently had some friends visit. I took some time in my office to write my newsletter for the week, and one of our friends asked me how I could do that, just sit down and write. I just do it. I've been doing it a long time. But I also don't get perfectionist about it. I am a pretty good writer (I hope it feels that way to you! Gosh that's a crazy thing to say in a book, right?), and I don't make a ton of mistakes. Because of this, I loosely proofread, and sometimes don't even have time to do that. Our friend informed me that if she saw a typo in a newsletter, she would be immediately turned off and not want to read anything again. I told her she was "not my people." Don't get me wrong; quality is important to me. I am a grammar snob. I've hired an awesome book editor. I did not do what many of my peers do and write the "good enough" book of short chapters with cliché information to just get it done. There, you see, I am a snob. Typos don't make me happy. But if someone doesn't want to get my information because of an occasional imperfection, I don't want to work with them. Period. (Our friend is a dentist, a great place to be a perfectionist, so no concern there!)

I love this quote by Vernon Howard, spiritual teacher and philosopher: "Never suppress yourself in order to hold, win, or influence another. When we are unreal, so are our rewards."

R – Ready. You also want your STAR client to be ready. Don't confuse this with their having loads of money sitting around to invest or already actively seeking you as a solution. Sometimes that's the case, but more often than not, if your expertise is working on the root causes of their problems, your client won't know that they need you, and certainly won't be looking for you. They are likely to be unaware that your solution exists. This is why you need to be skilled in asking the right questions and educating with your marketing. You want to work with a client who, after getting really clear through personal conversations or your marketing education, recognizes that the solution you offer is exactly what will help them make the shift, and that the shift is something that they really do want. They might still balk at investing, or have questions about details, the answers to which will satisfy their ego-mind, but deep down they are ready to make the change for their own reasons, and you are the person to help them do it.

Now that you've learned what the STAR client is, let's look a little deeper at why it so important to have one.

We All Long to Be Seen... and We Value It

So why do you want to choose a STAR client? Because just as in the story about Alexis, when you know specifically who your client is and what they struggle with, and you have a custom-crafted solution that is just for them, you can charge more for that very specific expertise.

Back when I was renovating my house in Cincinnati, I had two kitchens to demolish and re-create. I was on a very limited budget. I strolled through Home Depot more than once admiring the high-end cabinetry. In the end I purchased different cabinets for each kitchen. In the rental I installed maple-front cabinets that needed to be assembled. I actually really loved them. In my own kitchen I went with unfinished cabinetry and custom-stained them for me, using brown with colorful accents to recreate the Latin American vibe I so loved. I wanted my kitchen to truly represent me.

I was happy with my choices at the time, but coveted the ones in my friend's newly built custom home when I visited her, which were custom-designed by a high-end woodworker. They were a deep red tone, stark against the all-white home. They were absolutely gorgeous. And waaay beyond my budget.

According to Consumer Reports, stock cabinetry today is roughly $70 per linear foot. Custom cabinetry, on the other hand, is $500 per linear foot and beyond. The same is true for that custom evening gown or custom Rolls Royce. The same is true for your business. When your work FEELS custom tailored to your perfect audience, you can charge a premium.

For the same reason I wanted my kitchen to reflect me, your client wants an offering that really reflects them. We all want to be seen. And the mere experience of being seen has value.

Author Seth Godin said, "Great marketing completes the thought that's already happening in your prospect's mind," and I agree. If by knowing your client that well you are able to give voice to something they are already thinking — or better yet, something they haven't quite put their finger on for themselves — you've won them over.

My friend Laura is a business coach for massage therapists. She helps them add BodyMind Coaching to their work so that they can make more money in less time. As a former massage therapist herself, she knows the pain of being in that line of work. She knows the common complaints, like the wear and tear on the body of the therapist, and having to choose between making less money at a spa and going out on their own and having to market themselves. But she also addresses the pain they are NOT talking about. She addresses the hidden guilt they have about not loving this career that they were so passionate about when they started. She helps them understand that they are actually doing much more in their one-on-one sessions than just massaging people. They are often exchanging energy, hearing their hearts, and healing their souls. They know it, but often they've never heard anyone else acknowledge it. She also talks about the truth that they cannot imagine charging more than they do just to touch people, and that fear of all the regulations governing their industry makes them nervous to make claims about their value and keeps them from speaking their truths.

When Laura describes the pain her clients carry, I can feel it. When she describes it to them, they feel seen in a way they likely never have before. When you know someone better than they know themselves, they trust that you can solve their problem. Period. Laura has one of the best automated webinars I've ever heard about, which converts record numbers of prospects to clients. Not because she's been doing this forever – this was true right out of the gate, but because Laura understands the value of knowing her clients and seeing their pain. This has already made her loads of money ($80K from her first mini-launch), and her business is still quite new.

See your client on the surface, and read between the lines. Take the time to put the pieces together about who they are and what they are all about. The rewards are abundant. Let your client be seen, and in doing so, let them see you.

Claim Your Expertise

When you embrace your story and what you are naturally committed to and good at, and you take the time to understand how this addresses the thoughts, problems, and desires of your STAR client, you are working with the deep insight that helps you to claim your expertise.

One of the fastest ways to develop this deep expertise is to choose a STAR client who is simply an earlier version of yourself. If you have been in their shoes, it's easy to remember what it was like and talk about it. If you understand your own hopes, fears, desires, and pains, and are willing to talk about those things, you easily attract others who are in the same position. My most effective marketing campaigns are some version of me sharing my truth from my own experience, inner thoughts, and fears. People sometimes think that this will make them seem too vulnerable, or like they are not an expert, but it actually has the opposite effect.

What happens if your STAR client is *not* actually some version of you? Maybe you want to market to mothers because you have a passion for serving their kids, but you yourself are not a mother. Or perhaps you want to market your wellness coaching to a corporate audience, but you have never worked in the corporate world. Check your heart and confirm that the audience you want to reach is actually who you are called to serve. While it's true that a corporate client generally has more money to spend on you, if that is the main reason you're focused there you might be the victim of the "scarcity mindset," which ultimately will not serve you. Your business journey will be easier if you target a version of yourself.

That said, if you decide to target an audience that is different from you, prioritize gaining deep insight into the thoughts and feelings they experience. You'll need to do some market research.

For years in my corporate job I did market research for new-product development. We conducted both qualitative and quantitative research. Qualitative research is done with small numbers of people in your target audience (you may not know whether or not they are STAR clients until after you've done your research), and goes in-depth with them about how they view products or solutions like yours. Quantitative research is done with larger groups of people such that it can statistically represent the greater whole of your audience.

Market research is actually really fun. You love people — what better than to spend your time learning more about them. You, too, can do market research to learn more about your target audience and to be able to define very specifically your STAR client.

As I already mentioned, my favorite kind of market research is working with actual clients and making insightful notes about our work together that include the *exact words* my clients said. Particularly when I was in product-development mode, clients used the same or very similar words call after call after call (thank you, Universe.) This is informal qualitative research. I even coined the marketing message "The Great Entrepreneurial Flip-Flop" after hearing three clients in one week talk about "flip-flopping around" or feeling like they were "flopping all over the place." This message made me a solid seven figures before I decided I was ready to work with clients who were past the flip-flop stage.

It won't surprise you that my other favorite form of qualitative research is... *a retreat!* Have your participants share their thoughts or ah-ha moments throughout your retreat. Capture them in writing, on a flip chart, to review later for your marketing. As you're evaluating the progress of your participants, make concrete notes to use later. Be sure to evaluate which clients you love working with and use their insights and ah-has to guide your decision-making. You can even intentionally create an exercise to test out and get written feedback on a specific piece of content. For example, you can have them complete and turn in a written assignment about how they feel right after you've shared a certain emotional story or concept, and use that more emotional language in your marketing.

When I worked in the corporate world, we often conducted focus groups. We went with people to the grocery store to do their shopping, and we did a variety of collaging and storytelling exercises with them to get to the heart of not just what they did, but how they thought and felt. There's no reason why you can't do this with a group of people in your target audience! Invite them over and serve them pizza. Conduct a "workshop" with the sole intention of collecting research. Stop people on the street outside a local corporate head office and ask them what they think about the topic you're working in. Do whatever it takes! Remember, qualitative research always requires interpretation by the researcher. You'll use what they say, along with your intuition and ability to make the connections within what they say, to draw your conclusions.

You can also conduct quantitative research. This is generally done through surveying people in your target audience. You may have noticed that surveys are very popular right now in the world of online marketing. It's much better than stabbing in the dark. There is a book called *Ask,* by Ryan Levesque, that walks you clearly through one methodology. This is also a way to get specific language by using open-ended questions that allow people to answer in their own words, which you can then use in your marketing.

A couple of notes about research: It's important to know that when people are together in a room providing opinions about specific ideas or products, most lie. They don't intend to lie, but often a dominant personality in the room takes over and suddenly the whole room believes the same thing. Even a skilled facilitator can't always prevent this from happening. Those who are skilled at telling people what they want to hear intuitively do just that. Those who like to play devil's advocate will play that role whether or not it is how they actually feel! This is why my research team always tried to create contextual situations that allowed people to actually behave the way they would in real life (that is, a live retreat situation!). The same can happen in a survey. Responders do their best to give honest answers, yet they often have idealized ideas about how they would behave in a certain situation that don't necessarily match up with what they would actually do.

When doing quantitative research, keep in mind where you make your survey available. Depending on your audience and how you intend to reach them, those who are willing to take the time to complete a survey are not the same people who would pay for your services. Do your best to put your survey in front of people who might be your STAR clients.

The bottom line is that you want to be insightful about your STAR client and give voice to what they are thinking. When you establish yourself as the person who understands their problem, you position yourself as the person who can solve their problem.

Irrational Fears about Choosing

My very first website had two target audiences. Coming from a research/development and marketing background, I knew the importance of speaking directly to my audience. I had two buttons on my homepage: "I have a job" and "I'm an entrepreneur." If you're going to target two groups, this is the way to go about it. But the truth is that I was afraid to choose just one target client. And it created double work for me all the time. If I wanted to update a message I had to do it on two sites. I had designed a program for entrepreneurs and one for people in jobs; I just didn't know which was the right audience and I was afraid to choose. And I am not alone. My fears about choosing were the same kind that prevent others from doing so – irrational.

Fear That There Won't Be Enough

The first and most obvious fear is that you won't have enough clients if you target only one kind; that clients will somehow be hard to find. I recently did the math with a client who is a relationship coach. Her love and sweet spot is working with women who are in relationships that are not working and they have been ignoring that fact because they don't want to deal with the consequences. She helps them decide "Should I stay or should I go?"

She was worried that this client base was too specific, and that there wouldn't be enough of those people. Her goal was to work with ten clients privately at any given time. So we looked up the population of the U.S. (318 million) and began to break it down. Number of women, number of adult women, adult women in relationships, and our estimate of the number of those relationships that were unhappy or not fully actualized. As you can imagine, this was still a lot of women. Then we considered the personality types of the women who would be drawn to her style and approach. (Of course hers is the deep, root-cause approach of taking responsibility and looking within.) We estimated that three of the sixteen personality types outlined by the Meyers-Briggs Foundation would resonate with her approach. Again, all estimates. At the end of the day we ended up with about six million ideal clients in the U.S.

And she wanted ten of them. She wanted to ultimately develop offerings that could reach beyond these ten people, but to be financially successful by her definition required just ten out of six million to find her and say yes. Totally doable! Remember your abundance mindset!

Fear of Abandoning Someone Who Needs You

The second fear that might cause you not to choose is that there will be people you don't choose who really need you. You don't want to abandon people who might need your help! I quickly realized after conducting a few lunch-and-learn presentations that I don't enjoy going into the corporate environment to give presentations. I had discovered the world of entrepreneurship and I knew I fit there. I liked being around people who had control over their time and choices, and felt free to use it. I also found plenty of entrepreneurs who were not successful and carried loads of victim energy regarding their lack of success, so it's not that the grass is all greener; I just found I preferred working with entrepreneurs.

I also liked that entrepreneurs are flexible. Be sure to choose STAR clients who can accommodate your schedule. My corporate clients who were trying to figure out what they really wanted to do with their lives were generally available evenings and weekends, and also had a lot more trouble setting a schedule and keeping it. Having come from the corporate world and knowing how many people working there were not happy, or in their careers for the wrong reasons, I felt I couldn't rule those people out. After all, some of them wanted change, and how could I resist helping?

It's okay to work with clients from outside your target audience on a case-by-case basis when they are great STAR fits. But don't market to them. Create marketing focused on one type of person. Even if you offer a variety of services, determine whether those services can each be tailored to the same type of person.

I'm going to say something that might seem contradictory to everything I've said so far in this book. Hold on to your hats…

Nobody needs you.

That's right, nobody needs you. You aren't obligated to do this work. You aren't obligated to help anyone. This is one of the grand paradoxes of your work as a service-based entrepreneur. The work you do has chosen you. You have a deep desire to make an impact in the world. You must believe your work is important in order to get out of bed in the morning. But at the same time you must believe it's not so important so you can maintain the freedom to choose the work you want to do each day.

If you don't serve a certain audience, someone else will. They may not do it in your way; they may not even do it as well as you can; but there is someone there for the people you leave behind, and those people are meant to work with someone else in a different way to change their lives.

The fear of abandonment has been present in my life in all kinds of ways due to having felt abandoned as a kid when my parents divorced. We re-create the experiences we have energetically stored within us until we heal them. We also project those experiences onto others, whether they feel them or not. I guarantee that those I didn't choose to work with didn't feel abandoned by me. They didn't even know I existed. This fear was all my stuff, and I had to own it. Even now as I write this book for retreat leaders and those who want to be, I am leaving behind loads of great entrepreneurs I would have worked with in the past so that I can focus on making a huge impact in a specific arena.

The day I deleted one of those buttons from my website was a freeing one indeed.

Fear of Boredom

The other fear I had in choosing a STAR client was the fear of boredom. We think that working with one type of client to solve one type of problem sounds like the death of creativity. I get it. I resist routines as much as anyone. I love creativity and variety. I love to create just for the sake of creating. But it's not always profitable. That doesn't mean you shouldn't do it anyway (I do all the time), it's just not always smart business.

Here's what might surprise you: The more you narrow and focus, the more creative you get to be! This shocked me, too. When you are not focused on a specific client, you are spending your time thinking about general solutions for general problems. You have to, for lack of a better term, dumb down your work to reach multiple people. When you choose exactly who you are here to serve, you can actually put your brain power to work on how to serve them in a better, clearer, more creative way. Your work gets traction so much faster that you are able to play with many more clients.

And here's another piece of the creativity puzzle: Even though it might seem like all your work will be the same, each client is actually very unique, and it's a lot of fun tuning in to the nuances of what makes them different. You become a trend-spotter and a creator of the exact right tools for your people. I have personally found a great deal of creativity and freedom in this approach!

Who Is Your STAR Client?

What type of person are you here to serve? Be as specific as possible, as this will help you as you move into the next piece of your journey. Here are some questions to answer in addition to considering the STAR qualities – Smart, Tenacious, Aligned, and Ready:

- Do you like them? Would they be the type of person you'd want to go on vacation with?

- Does working with them allow you to work the schedule you want to work?

- Do they understand the value of investing in the outcome you provide? This could also be phrased as "Do they have money?" but I never believe in asking this way, as people surprise you with the resources they have when they desire an outcome.

- Do they gather in specific places online? In the real world? All things being equal, if you choose an audience that already gathers, whether in person or online, they will be easier to find and market to. What is great these days is that groups that don't otherwise have time to gather in person do get together on social media.

EXERCISE:

Karina C.
Leslie S-S
Diane E
Liv

STAR Client Profile

Profile your STAR client. When you know your STAR client, everything becomes easier: how to market to reach them, what content to include in your retreat, and, most important, how to offer your services in a way that makes them say yes! Use the following prompts as your guide:

1. What does your STAR client do for a living?

2. What are the demographics of your STAR client (age, gender, income, marital status, kids, etc.)? *35-60, F, M, $75K+*

3. What else is unique about your STAR client's life or work circumstances? *Successful, unhappy, off-purpose, searching*

4. What does your STAR client like to do for fun? *hike, nature,*

5. What does your STAR client spend most of their time thinking about? *physical* *how to fill the hole, find what's missing*

6. What does your STAR client regularly shop for? *self-help books* *clothes*

7. What does your STAR client splurge on? *Vacations*

8. What else does your STAR client invest in? *health + well-being spiritual growth*

9. What is the current pain/problem/frustration your STAR client is experiencing? *feel stuck, lost, something missing*

   - What do they think their problem is? *not living purpose* *clarity*
   - What does your unique perception tell you their problem really is? *not living passions or purpose*

10. What sorts of thoughts might your STAR client have when they think about solving this pain/problem/frustration? *confusing, overwhelming, scary*

11. What sorts of things does your STAR client currently do to either avoid, hide from, or attempt to solve their problem? Are these things effective? Why/Why not? *Read; figure it out themselves; hope*

12. What are your STAR client's biggest fears? *$ not reaching potential*

13. What would your STAR client most like changed?
Their joy + Soul fulfillment

Great work on choosing and defining your STAR client! Now it's time to have them pay you! This is so important to being able to market your retreat. Offering your services and asking for money is the focus of the next chapter.

Chapter 5

Offer It – How to Ask for Money for Your Gifts

Sarah was incredibly anxious. I could feel her vibration through the phone line. She was in the midst of all kinds of change. She had come to me because she knew she'd outgrown the business she created. She loved what she was doing but felt called to something more. She'd been working as a wellness coach for years, and having done that she now wanted to teach other women how to create a wellness business doing the work they love. Her own business had been a vehicle for her to spend more time with her kids as they grew, and she wanted to empower other women to have that same opportunity.

She also wanted to make more money. On some level she knew she was worth more and that all her years on the planet, in business and through other life experiences, had more value than what she'd been allowing herself to accept. Just shifting gears to become a business coach, however, had not automatically created a higher price tag.

It is a common misconception that people make decisions to become business coaches, rather than health coaches, relationship coaches, copywriters, or creative professionals, because they believe that people will pay more for business coaching. It is also a misconception that coaching is easy and doesn't require a lot of time. What those who go into business coaching often don't realize is that the VALUE they bring to their clients has to do with their alignment with the outcome they deliver. Choosing business coaching without that true alignment absolutely does not work.

While there is some truth to the idea that it's easier to justify investing a higher dollar in one's business than in one's health, that is not a reason to change course from doing the work you love. Because wherever you go, there you are, and you still have to deal with your inner game around receiving money.

When Sarah called for her coaching session, she was aligned with helping other women work from home. She'd just developed her first high-level offering. It was an investment of $6,000. She'd held a free strategy session the day before with a potential client, and that was the first time she'd quoted her price. The prospect's response was an upset, "Well, that's a lot of money! I can't afford that," followed by an abrupt exit from the conversation.

Then she had a session with a potential client who was a great fit. During the call the prospect revealed her deepest wishes to Sarah along with the honest truth of what was in the way. Sarah knew she could help her, but waffled a bit when she had to quote her price because she still felt shaky from the prior call. This time the prospect voiced a random objection that had nothing to do with money or anything they had been talking about; it came completely out of left field. Sarah was completely thrown off and ended the call feeling frustrated.

I don't remember the exact objection that was given to Sarah, but here are some I've heard in strategy-session calls: "My sister is getting divorced so it's a busy time." "I want to learn about social media first." And my personal favorite, "I'm keeping the money in my savings account to help my son buy his girlfriend an engagement ring when he's ready."

As we unpacked what had happened, I asked Sarah, "What were you thinking when the prospect gave you that objection?"

Sarah said, "I thought the idea was crazy and had nothing to do with the real issue."

I told Sarah that was a perfectly legitimate thought and asked her, "I'm just curious, why didn't you say that?"

So often in conversations about money and investing, and even in many coaching conversations in general, people don't say what they actually think. They hold back for a variety of reasons, attempting to say the right thing to get the person to buy, or because it just doesn't seem right to say the honest thing they're thinking. That's what had happened in Sarah's case. She didn't say what she was actually thinking because she was afraid she might upset the person.

Most of us don't like to upset other people, but the particular reason *why* we like to avoid conflict is unique. So I asked Sarah to share a bit more about what she was afraid of in that call. The person she'd talked with previously had gotten flustered and hung up. That had made Sarah feel shaky and on guard. She certainly didn't want that to happen again.

I asked her to remember the first time she had had that feeling. She was quickly taken back to her childhood when she lived in a constant state of fear of upsetting people. She would come home from school and spend time with her sister while waiting for her mom to come home. She would play and have fun, but as the time for her mother to come home drew near she would become hyper vigilant, trying to make sure everything was just right so her mom wouldn't get angry. Sometimes this worked well, but if it didn't her mom would yell and blame and lock herself in her room and not come out, sometimes for days. Once her mom was locked in her room, Sarah would then be responsible for taking care of the house and her sister. She'd been made to feel that the whole thing was her fault.

This happened for most of Sarah's childhood. She never knew what would set off her mom; it could be anything, but sometimes it involved money. As a result of this, Sarah has spent her life attempting to keep the peace, proving that she would never be the type of person to create that kind of unrest.

Fast-forward to the sales conversation in which she learned that the higher price point could upset and fluster people who really wanted to work with her. Based on how she'd seen the primary woman in her life react, of course Sarah would hesitate to say the thing that might upset the prospective client. She imagined the prospect hanging up the phone and spending days locked in her bedroom... and blaming Sarah for it!

Through the process of shifting this belief Sarah was able to see that rather than creating a problem, saying what she was actually thinking to her prospect could create a breakthrough – for both her *and* her prospect. (I use a handful of different tools in my programs to support clients in consciously embodying new beliefs.)

That prospect had her own pattern. She was likely accustomed to throwing out random excuses to confuse people. And those people probably didn't tell her the *truth*, so she got away with avoiding making the changes she needed to make. (I call this being "slippery.") Sarah had the chance to change that.

Lots of people talk about shifting beliefs and thinking positively. I remember when Stuart Smalley used this mantra on *Saturday Night Live*: "I'm good enough, I'm smart enough, and doggone it, people like me." Yet this kind of positive thinking doesn't actually work. In order to change a belief you must actually take a different action. You must give yourself a new experience. Figuring out where a pattern comes from makes you feel good. Saying affirmations makes you feel good. But they are not enough, *especially* with patterns involving money. The moment you recognize the pattern and the fear, you must give yourself a new experience that flies in the face of that fear.

Sarah called the prospect again and told her what she was actually thinking. She even let her know that she didn't say what she was thinking at the time because she didn't want to upset her, but realized that it was okay for the prospect to get upset because she had big dreams to fulfill, and that Sarah wasn't doing her any favors by trying to keep the peace. The prospect became her first $6,000 client.

Sarah went on to offer strategy sessions to the subscribers on her old business list, and she brought in two more of those $6,000 clients that same week. She reprogrammed her pattern of thinking regarding money and making people upset by speaking the truth in each of these sessions and finding the right clients to work with.

Learning to ask for and receive money is one of the very best ways to change your life. Period. I've watched it happen for countless clients. The pattern that keeps you from being able to do this is the pattern that keeps you from all kinds of other success in your life.

Offering your gifts takes courage. Offering your gifts for money takes faith. Let's explore!

Asking and Receiving

There is nothing more difficult, or that creates more vulnerability, than the process of asking and receiving, especially for women. But it's not *just* in relation to money. Women around the globe are willing to put themselves into any number of painful scenarios to get stuff done rather than ask for and receive support.

Yet we are meant to receive. Women make things happen through collaboration, and through giving and receiving. In recent years, as women have taken on masculine traits to participate in an economy that was primarily controlled by men, we've become much more "take charge" and have forgotten how to relax and receive. But you will be quickly out of business if you don't receive money for your services. For women to make the biggest change in the world, we need to run businesses in a more feminine, heart-centered, and collaborative way. And we absolutely need to master asking and receiving.

Years ago I bought a house that was in foreclosure (and it looked like it!). Just as I am able to see what's special about people, I was also apparently able to see what's special about a house, even amid the dirt and grunge, like the graffiti on the wall in the first floor foyer and the toilet that was growing so much it seemed it might walk away.

I'd been watching a lot of Home & Garden Television (HGTV) and I didn't think it would be too hard to whip that house into shape. The folks at HGTV could do it in a weekend, right? So surely I could do it in a summer!

I put an offer in on this house and took out a loan to purchase and also renovate. I made my plans, my timeline, and my budget, and I went to work. It was the period after my stint as a high school teacher, and I was working part time waiting tables at a diner. I'd head into work in the mornings sporting my lovely uniform polo shirt, and in the afternoons quickly change into my grungy army-green work pants and a tank top. Every spare moment I was tearing down walls, scraping wallpaper, or caulking windows and trim. Luckily this meant I had very buff arms! As the summer came to an end it became increasingly apparent that I was not going to finish the house when I had planned. I also realized I was going to lose my mind if I spent one more day alone with a caulk gun.

I didn't have the budget to outsource any more work – I'd already had the place rewired, I'd contracted out the bathroom remodel and window replacement, and also had a load-bearing wall removed. I couldn't throw any more money at the problems. I needed to ask for help, which terrified me.First of all, I'd been somewhat cavalier in my purchase of this home. I was smart and capable, and of course I could do this – just watch! Recognizing that I actually couldn't do what I thought I could was humbling. Admitting it to other people – whoa!

Second, I'd never really asked for help, at least not in an empowering way. I'd maybe "guilted" people into doing something with or for me in the past (I'd learned that from my mother). And I had created opportunities for others to help me and made them look like fun (fundraising party anyone?). And I had begrudgingly received help while pretending I didn't need it, like when a friend brought me chicken soup when I was sick.

But I knew I needed support with this house. I was renting an apartment across town with my friend who was meant to become my first-floor tenant. Every day that went by was a day we were each paying rent to someone else rather than her paying rent to me! I could have gone about getting help in ways similar to those listed above and remained the same closed-off person I'd been before, but I'd been doing empowerment training and working on my mindset. I saw the opportunity to truly ask and receive. I had no idea at the time that becoming that person would be so important to my future growth!

I called people I knew and shared vulnerably that I had taken on something I couldn't do alone and that it was hard to admit that and ask for help. I let them know that just sharing that with them was a breakthrough for me, and I thanked them. I invited them to contribute and provided specific options such as come over and help me paint the living room for a few hours. I let them know that it was perfectly okay to say yes or no, and that I was enjoying the opportunity to ask. I also asked them to think about what might be in it for them. In other words, I let them know that I wanted them to win, too, whether by returning the favor or giving them an opportunity for creativity and contribution.

Through this work I actually deepened relationships with people in ways I couldn't have imagined. By allowing them to help me, we connected at new levels. I was vulnerable, and I lived. And I had much more fun. I went on to live in that house for years, and the renovation created many lessons and opportunities for me. It was like a renovation of the soul.

We are so afraid of asking and receiving that we make all kinds of decisions to insulate ourselves from that experience. We avoid risks. We calculate and control. Yet that experience of having to ask and receive might be just what is needed to free us from our own traps.

When you get to where you actually need to ask for money... well, I love that place, because that's where the biggest growth can happen! And just like Sarah's relationship to upsetting others was personal to her, you have a unique relationship to what you're willing to receive. The breakthrough in asking and receiving is specific to you, but the opportunity is there to be had!

What Money Means

Money itself is inert. It's a small piece of paper that makes it possible to receive compensation from others. That is all. The emotion of money is entirely ours. Money can excite us and make us feel important. It can put fear into our hearts or make us feel selfish. None of that is the fault of money. It has everything to do with what we make money mean.

We each grew up with all kinds of messages about money. Before the age of seven, our conscious minds are not yet formed. This means we have no ability to accept or reject ideas that flash across our minds. We are imprinted or programmed by how we feel about what our parents feel and do about money.

Did your parents view money as scarce? Then you likely inherited this belief. Did they do things they didn't want to do in order to earn it? Did they enjoy paying bills, or complain about it? Was it okay for you to ask for things you wanted, or were you told that money doesn't grow on trees?

What did you have to do to earn money as a kid? Did you have a specific, predictable way to earn it, such as defined chores or an allowance, or did you have to ask and hope? Was money given freely? Were you expected to behave a certain way because your family had money?

What did you learn about people who have money? Were they called selfish, greedy, or evil, or were you encouraged to get to know them? What were you taught about people who didn't have money? Were you encouraged to feel sorry for them? To give them more? To judge them as less?

I enjoy creating experiences for people in which they get to see what's really going on for them. Thinking about what you make money mean is a great start. But actually EXPERIENCING your own beliefs and judgments in action is a whole different ball game.

In my very first group-coaching program I mailed each of my clients a $5 Starbucks gift card. The accompanying note asked them to use the card to buy coffee for someone in line at their local Starbucks. Sounds simple, right? Yet you wouldn't believe what this simple exercise stirred up for them. There were a few who did it happily and with ease, but *almost everyone* had some resistance to the exercise. They worried about what people would think of them for buying them coffee. Their fear of the "Who do you think you are?" judgment was a mirror of their own judgment of people with an abundance of money.

Most quickly became aware of their decision-making in regard to giving this gift. They assessed who in line most needed it, or who in line least needed it, and gave accordingly – some giving to the person who looked the poorest, some giving to the wealthiest-looking person because it would surprise them the most.

Several people in each group delegated their duties by giving it to the barista and asking them to award the coffee, or by passing it on in the drive-thru line. Most did not want to have a live human connection with the person to whom they were giving the coffee.

Considering the level of vulnerability my clients felt regarding a gift of coffee, you can imagine how it would be amplified in asking for money from someone they were going to serve! Think about your own vulnerability. Many entrepreneurs choose to survive this process by undercharging. Like Sarah, when they shift their rates to ones they can easily live on, they want to hide.

The Sheer Panic of Asking for Money

For years I offered a money retreat in which I used a modification of an exercise that was given to me by my mentor. Participants were given a "game," with a winner and a prize. The game was to generate money. The rules were initially vague, and got more specific as the evening progressed, but in general they were to find a way to get people on the street to part with their money. In the beginning they could sell their usual business services. Avenues such as social media were not off the table. In round two those options were taken away, requiring them to be more creative. They played in teams, both for safety and to reveal how groups influence individual actions.

I could write an entire book on the experiences that stemmed from those seven retreats, but instead I'll summarize some of what I noticed. Note that the exercise is about asking and receiving, period.

In every single group, every single time, as I announced and shared the rules of the game, panic ensued. Some people panicked quietly with smiles on their faces. Others loudly objected to the whole idea. I let them know that their future depended on their winning the game. Whatever kept them from winning the game would also keep them from asking for money in their business. It sounds dramatic but I meant it. When they discovered they would have to talk to people, and in particular talk to them about money, they begged to do anything else. For almost everyone the panic was not about money but about "What will people think of me?"

Getting Ready to Get Ready

Just as in business, many teams spent an hour or more brainstorming ideas about how to generate money and creating complicated plans requiring many supplies and resources to get started. This mirrored exactly the millions of business owners who spend time safely behind their laptops rather than talking with potential clients. They wanted everyone on the team to buy in, and each person's fears were contagious. For every great idea there was someone on the team who was afraid of that idea, which spiraled the team down.

What Do I Have That Is of Value?

Whether they had an elaborate planning process or an on-the-fly style, every single team spent energy trying to determine what they could offer that was of value. Earlier in the day we'd spent a good hour in a conversation about value, and had brainstormed a list of what has value. The list included everything from money, time, and knowledge to experience, connection, joy, play, etc. When under stress, this list flew out the window, and each person went into their own form of hell, asking themselves, "What could I possibly offer that would have value here?" Based on that question, each team formulated a plan. Some sold their services – a coaching session, an astrological reading, a health consult, a massage. Inevitably at least one team would have a strategy to sell hugs. Others planned to use money to buy something of value and resell it. The more complicated the strategy, the less money the team generated.

Who Will or Won't Part with Money?

As with the Starbucks exercise, in each retreat we learned a lot about how people decided whether or not their prospect had money. A large amount of energy was spent trying to decide where people with money would be. Often the people who looked like they had the most money were the least generous. Was this true, or a projection of the participants' own belief systems playing out?

One team received a significant amount from a group of recovering heroin addicts who were living in a halfway house. The team approached them because they were dressed in suits. Teams that were most successful targeted people most likely to have cash, like servers and cab drivers, but most teams didn't ask these people because they work so hard for their money.

Participants had concerns about their own appearance and how it would affect whether or not people would give them money. If they were well-dressed and felt put together, would people want to give? What stories would others make up about them and why they were asking for money? In one retreat, an attendee who had flown to Baltimore from another country arrived with just twenty dollars in her pocket to spend for the weekend. As she walked the streets, she encountered many people begging. She told us she felt sorry for those people and was worried about what they thought of a rich white girl walking by them. We lovingly pointed out that people on the street asking for money were likely much richer than she was. Because she had nice clothes that perhaps her parents had bought for her, and she had traveled from another country to be there, she felt rich. Yet she had no plans for how she would eat dinner that night, and she had much to learn from the people who understood how to receive. She struggled in the exercise because if she really became present to – or embraced or acknowledged – how much she actually *needed* money it would mess with her beliefs about her own identity. This happens often for people who move from being in a job to being in business. In a job you talk about money just once, or possibly once per year, when you negotiate the amount you are willing to receive for your services. When that is done, the money simply comes. In business it's a regular daily conversation, one that people often prefer to ignore.

Is It for a Good Cause?

Many participants wanted to know what would happen to the money they collected. They had grand stories about how they could not "in good conscience" ask for money if they didn't know what was going to happen to that money, as if they would be thieves if someone gave them five dollars that wasn't for a good cause. The moralistic high road cost them the game. The group did indeed choose a charity to send the money to each time, but they did not know this outcome at the start, and it stopped many people.

In round two I told them that the money would go to a good cause, which was still left open to interpretation. Many groups invented a charity to tell people the money was going to, as they did not want to ask for money just for themselves. But could they visualize personally living a great life as a good cause?

Following the Rules

The rules of the game were vague on purpose. The rules of entrepreneurship are generally vague as well. By definition you are creating and profiting from something that didn't exist before, that you created. There are no rules! It is amazing to watch a group of grown adults who are in charge of their own lives and thoughts and actions be stopped by rules that don't even exist! At any point a true leader could have emerged and defined the rules in a way that suited them, as there was nothing stopping them from doing so, but no one, I repeat, *on one* ever did. What rules have you invented about money that stop you from coloring outside the lines and being a leader in your own space?

Figuring It Out and "The Answer"

Halfway through the game, I let them know that there was an answer to the game. Just letting them know this elevated their thinking and caused them to take a step back and look at the big picture. Still, very few people found the answer.

There is a distinct difference in how people approach the game and how they envision winning. I learned this from my mentor, and it changes everything in terms of asking and receiving.

Each team expended loads of energy trying to "figure out" the right thing to offer — that would have value; that the people in that environment would want to pay for; that would entice and engage; that would reach the people with money, etc. (Do you recognize this in your own business?) They wanted to figure out the right thing so that they would look good, be clever, be right, win the game, sound smart, avoid looking stupid, etc. I guarantee you're doing this too. (I still do at times!)

But "the answer." is simply to ask. Do not be attached to having the right answer, but instead ask for the right answer. You have to ASK YOUR AUDIENCE what they actually value! Here is the question my mentor gave me that changed everything:

"What would have you give me $100 and feel good about doing it?"

I repeat, because it's worth repeating: "What would have you give me $100 and feel good about doing it?" This could also be phrased, "What would make you give me $100 and feel good about doing it?" however the word *make* implies a sort of force, whereas *have* implies more of a willingness.

It's not rocket science, right? If you ask people what they want, they will tell you. If you ask people what they value, they will tell you. But you have to connect. You have to risk whatever they might say in response. You have to trust your ability to then say yes or no with power in order to open yourself up enough to ask. (I once had two men at a bar tell me that sexual favors was the path to their pocketbook.)

We like to remain in control of our asking and receiving because it makes us feel safe when we have defined the rules. "I'll give you X for Y dollars," period. You'll learn in *Retreat and Grow Rich* that I am a fan of having clear and defined packages and offerings, so I don't recommend custom tailoring for each person unless that really lights you up. But you can offer the same thing to different people FOR DIFFERENT REASONS. Understand their personal reasons for the work they want to do with you. Ask and be open enough to hear the response. This is always a vulnerable act. In business, vulnerability is strength.

ALIGNED Selling

Just as in the money game, the answer when it comes to asking for and receiving money in your business is asking people what has value for them.

I teach an approach I call ALIGNED Selling. It's a distinct course I offer in my client programs, and could fill a book itself, but the primary message is that *selling* your services is discovering the natural alignment between what your prospect wants and what you offer.

Most people don't know, or *aren't present to*, what they actually want. So the way to "sell" is not to tell someone about what you offer and ask them if they want it. The conversation should uncover what they actually want (desired destination), get a clear view of where they are now (the pain at the bus stop), identify the gap, and help them decide whether or not they are committed to closing that gap. If your retreat or other offering can close that gap, then and only then should you share the nuts and bolts with them.

Blair Enns adds to this conversation in his book *The Win Without Pitching Manifesto* when he shares that the intent of your sales conversation should not be to have your prospect buy, but rather *"to have the prospect form the intent to solve their problem."* When you can expertly guide your prospect to see their problem and decide to solve it, your retreat or program will be the natural solution they choose.

Here's a brief overview of the flow of the A.L.I.G.N.E.D. Selling conversation with some brief prompts you can use:

A – Ask (what they want – go beyond the pat answer)
- Tell me about your goal(s)
- What would achieving that goal make available?
- If you had a magic wand and could change one thing in your life/business/health right now, what would that be, and why?
- If you had that, then what?
- Why is that important to you?

L – Listen (for what they really want or need – read between the lines)

- What I hear in what you're sharing is that you really desire X.
- Wow, that sounds like it's really important to you.
- You really want that result so that you can actually have X. How true does that feel to you?

I – Impact (of where they are now)

- What's life like for you now?
- Tell me about a typical week in your life today.
- If what you really want more than anything is X, what's going on for you now that you don't have that?

G – Gap (between where they are and where they want to be – get them present to it)

- What do you think is in the way of your having what you want?
- What's it like knowing you would really like X, but instead having Y?
- How long has this been going on?
- How long have you had this goal?
- If six months or a year from now this hasn't changed, then what?

N – Now What?

- Now what?
- What would you like to do about it?
- What are you willing to do to change this?
- *(Your prospect might actually ask if you can help them, inviting you then to share about your services.)*

E – Empower (share your services and empower them to choose)

- Would you like to know what I think?
- May I share my recommendation with you?

- The program I recommend that is perfect for what you want to accomplish is...
- *(Share the overall outcomes and structure of your program – don't go into too much detail here.)*

D – Decision

- Would you like to do this?
- When would you like to get started?
- My next opening is X. Will that work for you?
- I'd love have you at my retreat / I'd love to work with you. What do you think?
- How would you like to pay for that?
- *("Maybe" and "I'll think about" are not true decisions. Neither is "I can't afford it." Empower your client to make a decision about what they actually want to do rather than allowing their circumstances to dictate their options.)*

Letting People Be Uncomfortable

Just as Sarah learned, offering your transformational services, and especially being paid well for them, often makes people uncomfortable. You are likely learning about retreats because you really do want to shift some of the current cultural assumptions on our planet. Whether it is the way we as a culture deal with health or communication, or how we treat our kids, our planet, ourselves, or our relationships, there is something that doesn't feel right to you. You've identified something that causes people pain, and see that if they could transform, the planet would shift. This is usually the perception of the transformational entrepreneur.

And here's the issue with being a transformational entrepreneur who wants to save people from experiencing pain: you will try to prevent your clients and prospects from experiencing pain. Pain, or discomfort, is the number-one motivation for transformation. It's nice think that we transform because we want to be better people, and sometimes that's the case, yet it is more often that our discomfort becomes so intense that we're forced to take our transformation into our own hands. And guess what: You want clients who are in pain and ready to take their transformation into their own hands!

Many coaches will tell you that to be a masterful transformational leader you have to get comfortable with being uncomfortable, and you have to get comfortable with allowing, and even causing, other people to be uncomfortable. Shifting reality does not happen by having nice conversations that please everybody. Being a transformational leader requires becoming okay with people's feathers being ruffled by the conversations you lead.

These conversations include talking about and asking for money. This topic has been taboo in our culture for a long time, but if you want to shift your experience of financial abundance, you have to come out of hiding when talking about money. You serve your potential clients best by asking them questions like these:

- When you say you can't afford this, what do you mean, specifically? *no $ ~~for this at~~ all, or no $ for this?*
- What are you spending money on that you could shift in order to prioritize money for this decision?
- If money were not an issue — if the money fell into your lap tomorrow — would you use the money to invest in this?
- What is it costing you not to get this support to make this change?
- What agreements do you have with your spouse or partner about money?
- What do you think your spouse or partner would say about this decision to invest in yourself?

Objecting to spending the money is a way to disguise what is really going on. Because there is an unspoken agreement in our culture not to talk about money, people who consider investing in their transformation often use money to deflect from the real issue at hand, which is getting uncomfortable in service of changing their lives. It's important for you to become strong enough to be able to ask the questions that make people uncomfortable enough to make a change. There is a whole retreat to be experienced around this, and I've led it many times.

You've chosen to be a transformational leader. Or perhaps that work has chosen you. To walk this path you will make people uncomfortable. You should endeavor to be so grounded in your value system and your truth that you will stand for them even when it makes people nervous. That's the path you've chosen.

There are days I wish to hop off this path. If you're having that thought, I get it. But because you're reading these words, there is likely some part of you that is lit up by the responsibility that comes with this leadership. And to that part of you I want to say THANK YOU. You've got this.

Now let's put these practices and mindsets about giving and receiving into action!

EXERCISE:

Money Flow

I challenge you to give away twenty dollars to a stranger within the next week. Notice the thoughts and beliefs that surface. Give it to them directly rather than avoiding the intimacy of the exchange. Notice the value *you* receive from the exchange. How might this correlate to the value your new clients will receive by parting with their money *before* they even start to work with you!?

I highly recommend you immediately begin having ALIGNED Selling conversations every chance you get so you master asking and receiving. Work with at least six clients in some capacity, be it for one day or three months, before marketing your retreat. That being said, you are going to begin planning your retreat! In the next chapter you start your content mapping!

Chapter 6

Content Is King... Sort Of

"But I don't have any real content," Kate said as we were mid-VIP-Day via Skype. I knew this wasn't true, but I played along. Kate was one of those people whose gifts just oozed out of her pores. You could feel that she was deep and smart and could likely do just about anything she set her mind to. She'd been a yoga instructor, a therapeutic play practitioner, a Reiki master, a professional clown, a world traveler, and more. She was at the point at which she wanted to pull all of her tools together under one umbrella and finally make some money with them. She was a natural coach and healer of old wounds. She intuitively knew how to work with people to get the outcome they wanted, whatever it was. This was part of her gift and strength – and also part of her problem. This is true for many coaches, consultants, and healers. They know they can help with pretty much anything, so how to decide which things to focus on in their retreats?

Every other week Kate had a new idea for a program, retreat, or offering she could create, and the abundance of ideas was clearly getting in the way. Even though she could envision all of these things, she believed she had no content because she hadn't actually created it yet. But if you can envision it, you can create it. She needed to choose a vision!

During our time working together she had honed in on women entrepreneurs as her target audience. She liked the experience of meeting them, they had a lot in common with each other, and she was always inspired by their courage in running businesses. She had a really clear picture of her STAR client. Based on looking at her own story and life experiences, she knew that the people she was most passionate about serving were people like herself who'd had experiences in their early lives that made them feel different, weird, or left out. She'd felt ostracized for a variety of reasons, including having older parents, going to church on Sundays, being left out of the Sardines games in the schoolyard, and being exceptionally smart. She knew the pain that separation could cause, and even as a grown woman was constantly trying to tone it down to fit in, yet feeling like a fake for doing it. She wanted to help others overcome that and claim their weirdness.

She had no shortage of ideas about how to help people to do this. She had done it unofficially for lots of people she'd met. She was a natural at helping people see what they couldn't see.

But what *was* her content? She needed to understand what it was that this STAR client really wanted that was practical and tangible and would allow her to get in there and guide them to heal their shame and claim their uniqueness. What was the "gateway" that would invite them in to her world?

She finally settled on guiding her clients to understand, specifically, why other people buy from them. She named her program Beacons, and her retreat Beacons LIVE, and it was all about digging into why people pay you. This work would require them to see all parts of themselves, including the ways they were faking it to fit in and the weirdness they had chosen to bury. The weirdness was actually what their clients loved about them and why they wanted to be around them. It was like the "Own It" work we did in chapter 3, but with a spin on looking at the way they were being perceived by others. The program would help people market themselves, embrace their value, raise their rates, and more.

As soon as Kate chose this focus she got excited because she knew it was something she could deliver. She began to make sales calls. With this specific outcome identified, she wrapped her mind around it and identified herself differently during these sales calls. It also became clear what she would do in her High-Level Program. She now had a sense of just where she was leading people and how she could weave the different tools in her toolkit into her work. Not only did she begin filling her first retreat, but she began selling her High-Level Program as well – for £18,000! Quite a raise from teaching yoga!

In this chapter my goal is to help you to gain clarity about what to actually *do* with your clients, and in what order, so that you can make decisions about what to include in your RICH Retreat, your High-Level Program, and your Gateway Program.

Let's get started.

Articulating the Transformation

You've chosen your STAR client. Hopefully you've taken some time to capture your insight in the STAR Client Profile from chapter 4. Now let's look at how you actually MARKET to those STAR clients and use all that insight to help them recognize you as the person to help them transform.

There are two main things to focus on in articulating the transformation your clients can expect: the PAIN of where they are now and the BENEFITS of being at the destination. To do so you need to understand the specific discomfort they're feeling and where you need to take them. Knowing these two things in great detail gives you everything you need to identify the transformation you empower, and market your business successfully.

As we covered in the previous chapter, no matter how specific your audience is, there is an abundance of potential STAR clients. Close your eyes and picture these people lined up at the bus stop. (Yes, now open your eyes so you can keep reading.) They are waiting for a bus to pick them up and take them to their destination. You are the driver of that bus. Working with you is their ticket from the pain they are experiencing at their bus stop to all the benefits at the destination where you are taking them. How do you help them know that they need to get on your bus?

The tricky part is that they aren't just standing still lined up in an orderly fashion; they're going about their lives in pain, and many don't even know they're supposed to be at the bus stop. In some area of their lives they are experiencing something other than what they want to experience, and they are ready to find a solution that takes them to a new destination.

This is true for you, too. Even if almost all areas of your life are going great and you feel happy overall, there is always an area in which you'd really love to make a change. Maybe your pants are a bit too tight, there is a chronic pain you've been tolerating, your business has taken a turn, or your relationship with your new boss isn't quite what you'd like it to be. Whatever the issue, we all have pain that we expertly ignore, avoid, or bury every single day. We are all at the bus stop.

While you might not be actively seeking solutions for every painful thing in your life (if you were, you would likely never get anything done!), if a solution finds its way to you and you can recognize it as a solution that is packaged specifically to meet your need, you will likely reprioritize to grab that solution.

For example, if you are walking through life with back pain, and you do not believe in surgery, and the bus pulls up with a marquee that says "Heal Back Pain Without Surgery," you are likely to pay attention. Even if you have no plan or budget set aside for healing your back pain, if skillful and truthful marketing causes you to believe that result is possible you will quickly rearrange your priorities and pocketbook and go for that solution. In this example, healing your back pain is the benefit at the destination. Fear of surgery is the pain at the bus stop. "Heal Back Pain Without Surgery" expertly weaves both the pain and the benefit into one statement, which is awesome.

It can be hard to weave that concisely, but you don't need to. Here's what you need to map out first:

- The top three to five PAINS your STAR client is currently experiencing at their bus stop
- The top three to five BENEFITS your STAR client wants to experience at the destination

You want to be able to say, "Hey, STAR client, I know you are feeling this, this, and this, and I get how hard that is. Hop on my bus, and together we'll get you to *here*, where instead of experiencing that pain you'll be able to have this, this, and this for the rest of your life!"

That is the crux of marketing every single part of your business – your HLP, your RR, and your Gateway, as well as any free resources or training you provide.

Different variations on these core pains and benefits can be used to engage potential clients at different stages of the journey. Take time to get clear about them. Take a stab at them even if you're not sure. You'll refine them as we walk through the rooms of your castle in the next section, and you'll refine them further as you work with your clients.

Content Mapping – The Rooms in Your Castle

Just like Kate, you have loads of content in your mind. You may not have written it down or recorded it in neat modules with workbooks and PowerPoint slides – no problem. What you see, believe, and know has huge value, and it is indeed content. In this section I provide guidance in how to think about your content and how to map it out in such a way that you can see it and feel it and make decisions about what goes where in your series of offerings.

Where a lot of people go wrong is not putting all the things they would like to teach and share into a context that can help their clients understand why they need them. For example, I've been working with Stacy, who uses all sorts of healing modalities. She knows which modality to use when, and shifts from one to another with ease. Her website listed all the modalities and individual sessions someone could buy, yet there was no sense of guidance about how it actually worked or what to expect. It was a smorgasbord of healing modalities with no place to start. Fortunately she'd been marketing herself in person, and people knew they needed to work with her anyway!

Stacy had created a multiple-six-figure business this way. But it required that she always show up live and promote herself. Her business didn't have a life of its own through structured content. And her content is healing, which isn't really content if you think about it!

You can bring in clients and earn great money by showing up and teaching whatever comes to mind and asking people to buy. People will feel your energy and want to work with you – IF YOU ASK THEM! Many entrepreneurs create some level of success by sharing whatever heartfelt solution comes to mind, and their clients love it; but their potential clients have no idea what steps to take to make a decision to work with them because there is no structure or clear path for saying yes. Put what you know and believe into a format that feels tangible and accessible to them. Begin by deciding which of these three camps you are in:

1) You have worked with clients already and some have been STAR clients.
2) You have worked with clients already but none have been STAR clients (maybe you're changing your focus or upping your definition of "Smart," the S in S.T.A.R.).
3) You have not worked with clients yet.

If you've worked with STAR clients already, I want you to think about your three favorite clients. Write their names down on a piece of paper, ideally as the headers of three different columns.

If you're in one of the other two camps, I want you to *imagine* your three favorite clients. It's a little more work for you, but I know you have an active, solid imagination! Start with imaginary client number one. Think of someone you know personally, or perhaps a character on TV or in a movie, who you intuitively know you could help. Perhaps it's that friend whom keeps staying in the job she hates because she's afraid to let go of the security. Or the colleague who keeps trying different diets but has never stopped to look at the real reason she uses food to hide her feelings. Get a really clear picture of this person. Write their name at the top of column one. If they are completely imagined, give them a name.

As an example, I once wrote a whole marketing campaign to a woman named Jessica who is thirty-two years old and lives in Louisville, Kentucky. She works for a marketing consulting firm that is owned by a friend who hired her because he knows how brilliant she is. She really wants to get out of that corporate grind. She likes her job, yet she knows she's meant to make a bigger difference. Her friend acknowledges her talent, but doesn't know the whole of her and doesn't necessarily let her do her job the way she wants to.

In her spare time Jessica trained as a yoga instructor, and she's been following a yogic lifestyle for a couple of years. She deeply wishes she could get everyone at the consulting firm to see what she sees about bringing more of a yoga mindset to work. She wonders if she might be able to go out on her own and use what she's learned to help people do this, but she doesn't see anyone else doing anything like that so she has no idea whether or not it will work. She needs a lifeline to help her believe.

Jessica isn't real. But you can likely relate to some of what Jessica has experienced. (If she were real, she'd love to get her hands on this book!) She is a combination of various clients I've had, and my vision of where someone might be when they connect with me. If you haven't yet worked with a STAR client, ask yourself who's your Jessica? Get that picture in your head.

Once you've made up your Jessica, invent another and another — friends, colleagues, TV characters, or totally imaginary people. Put their names at the top of the next two columns. Three STAR clients will help you create a holistic picture of your content. That said, if you have *one* imaginary client and you are clear about that person, you can choose to roll with just one.

Now, one client at a time, walk with them through the steps they will take to get from the pain they are in to the destination you will take them to. How will you guide them to the transformation? It can feel tedious, but this is a worthwhile investment of your time. One by one, step by step, think through what that person needs to KNOW, REALIZE, DISCOVER, CHANGE, or ACT UPON to create the transformation they desire. These are the steps of transformation for your STAR client.

You can do this in your three columns or grab a big flip chart and create three columns, writing the steps of transformation on individual Post-it notes, which will allow you to sort them in the next step. (I once heard that big ideas deserve big paper, and I find this to be true. ☺)

If you get hung up about what your transformation steps are, don't look for one right way to do it; what's most natural for you is the best way. That said, here are a few sample approaches:

You might take an "insight category" approach. If someone wants to lose weight, the first thing they might need is *insight* about why they carry weight, then *insight* about what they are afraid of, followed by a *decision* to lose weight, then *insight* about a physical activity that works for them and *insight* about a whole-food diet, wrapping up with *insight* into how to get support. Some of these are personal insights, others they might get from specific training that you provide. You might find that each of your three clients takes a slightly different path. That's okay because we'll be looking for the commonalities.

Other approaches you can take, or things to think of as you map out your steps, are:

- What I would teach them (including the order in which to do so)
- Things for them to master (specific skills they should learn)
- Types of sessions (do you first do a reading followed by a numerology session?)

Spend some time mapping out what you do with each of these three clients. I like to use Post-it notes on the wall, but you can also draw a chart on your paper similar to this one:

	CLIENT 1	CLIENT 2	CLIENT 3
STEP 1	insight		
STEP 2	Law of Att		
STEP 3	passions		
STEP 4	action		
STEP 5	accountab.		
STEP 6… ETC.			

The next step is to take a big-picture view of what you mapped out to look for trends among the three clients. What do you do with every client no matter what? What do you do with some and not others that makes the process more customized? Which elements must happen in a particular order and which can happen in any order? Now use these insights to map out a process that can be used as a guideline for all your clients.

You might want to have a friend or mentor work with you on this piece of the puzzle, as other people can sometimes see the method to your madness in a way that you can't see on your own because it's too instinctive to you. When we do this exercise in my retreats, participants often look at their work and say, "See, I told you I didn't have any content," or "This doesn't make any sense," but in reading their Post-it notes and asking a few questions I can quickly identify the system or process they follow.

At this point you might have a three-step process or a twelve-step process. Your goal is to use this process to define what I call "the rooms in your castle."

Let's Take a Castle Tour

Earlier we established that you are a bus driver. You are driving up to the bus stop with a really clear marketing sign on the front of your bus that distinguishes the destination in a way that your STAR client can understand. For example, two buses are heading to the greater Los Angeles area, one is labeled "Disneyland" and the other "Hollywood." These two buses will likely attract different types of riders even though they are going to essentially the same place.

Now let's change the scenario. You aren't actually driving the bus. You're the king or queen, after all; you wouldn't drive the bus (unless of course you wanted to!). So imagine that someone else is driving your bus with your marketing sign on it. They are saying to the folks at the bus stop, "Hop on and get a taste of this transformation," and driving people to your castle.

Why a castle? Because the moment they know you are a king or queen and you live in a castle, they are going to want some of that. They want to come in and see what you have! This puts you in an abundant frame of mind!

I'm not going to get too deep into front-end marketing strategies, but let's just say that they get drawn in – they cross the drawbridge, if you will – because they sampled an elegantly crafted taste of the work you do that you've given away for free, which has been delivered by your bus driver, who gave them a handy web link to an opt-in page... er... I mean a secret code to cross the drawbridge. So by the time they reach the front door of your castle, they already know that they like and trust you, and they want to get inside! (At one of my retreats we toured an actual castle, developed the content around the analogy of the castle, and it kind of stuck!)

You offered them some free content of some sort (ebook, audio file, video training, mini-course, quiz, etc.) by naming their pain and the destination they desired, and this enticed them to get on the bus, get driven to your castle, and cross the drawbridge. Now you invite them in to work with you. Depending on the type of castle you want to run – exclusive, benevolent, etc. – they might have to pay to get in or you might give them a mini-tour of a room in your castle for free (like a free webinar or workshop, for example). If the experience of entering the front door of your castle is sufficiently awesome, invite them to buy more at this point. This is where your RICH Retreat comes in. You will design your retreat in chapter 7. Right now you just want to understand your castle.

Just as when you invite someone to visit your home for the first time, you won't be taking your client straight to the bedroom. And you aren't going to give your newly engaged clients full rein in your castle. You will guide their experience.

Your paying clients don't just get to see the grand ballroom on the first floor where sometimes the whole village comes to play; they get to tour the second floor of your castle, which is more exclusive. This is where the bulk of your real work gets done. Imagine that there are a handful of rooms on the second floor. While your castle is certainly grand, four to six rooms is just the right amount. Each of these rooms contains pieces of your content or a step in your process. Define these rooms by looking at the way you outlined your work with clients in the exercise above. How would you group the steps in your process into "rooms"?

You can think of the rooms as the steps, pillars, keys, core concepts, main outcomes, etc. Establishing the rooms of your castle helps make the work you do accessible to your clients and identifies in which of the rooms your RR should be located.

When I was marketing business coaching, before discovering the wonderful world of teaching people to host transformational retreats, my castle had five rooms:

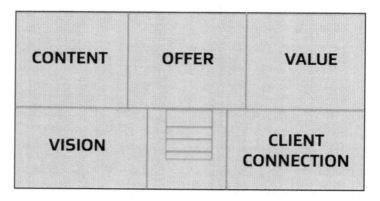

I worked with people in these five areas as they established their successful and aligned businesses:

- Vision: What is it they truly want to create and why?
- Content: What do they teach and how do they help their clients get results?
- Offer: How do they position their services and ask people to buy them?
- Value: How do they price their services, energetically align with those prices, and become confident about the value of what they offer?
- Client Connection: What marketing vehicles will they use to meet clients?

Establishing these five rooms in my castle allowed me to make decisions about what to talk about and in what order, and more specifically how my RR fit into my mix of offerings.

When I did the three-client exercise outlined above I found myself with ten to twelve steps each client went through in the development of their aligned business. I then bucketed these steps into the five categories of Vision, Content, Offer, Value, and Client Connection. From there I chose to focus my RR on the room in my castle called Value, primarily helping people own their value and be empowered to raise their rates.

Establishing the rooms of your castle is foundational to the rest of the decisions you make about your retreat-based business. In the exercise at the end of this chapter you'll define them more specifically. That being said, don't overthink them. Take your best guess. Look at the steps your three clients moved through to get from the pain to the benefits at the destination, and use those to inspire your four to six rooms, or "pillars."

You can always change the rooms around if you begin working with them and find that they're not quite right. There might be several different ways you can group your steps into rooms. Trust yourself and take your best guess! You can't get it wrong if you make decisions that align with your heart!

As we work through the coming chapters I will refer back to the rooms of your castle. These rooms are the foundation of each of your three core programs. When your clients work through the second floor of the castle they will get to the destination they desire! These rooms are a guide for you to determine what content goes in your HLP, what goes in your RR, and the secret sauce to put in your Gateway! ☺

Concept over Content

I want to share a bit about what I've learned about content. I called this chapter "Content Is King... Sort Of" for a reason. Understanding where you take people and what they experience on the journey there is important to your sense of confidence in your work and your client's sense of confidence in you. If you have unique content – a unique way of talking about a topic or a fun way to help someone learn – it helps you stand out. And it makes it easy for people to spread the word about your programs.

In my corporate job I used to create models – nothing more than representations, usually visual, of how something happens or how something works. We created models to represent human behavior. This is always trickier than creating physical models – for example, a model of a car – because human behavior is complex, and distilling it is an art. It happens to be an art that I have practiced. Not all my clients have practiced such modeling, but they know they can come to me and spew out all the things they think about and care about and believe in, and I can turn it into a model. It might be a flowchart, a cycle, or an acronym that makes them memorable. It's not necessary to represent your content graphically; for example, you might just use four bullet points. Yet anything you can do to help your audience remember your content and know how to apply it helps.

You do not need a lot of content. I repeat, *you do not need a lot of content.* Some of my retreats require no content whatsoever other than a good story. The work you've done thus far is 90 percent of the work needed to create a multiple-six-figure business. If you know who your STAR client is, the pain they are experiencing, and where you want to take them, that is the lion's share of what you need to market and sell your services. So, content is king... sort of.

You are an intuitive person. That is part of what drew you to this book. When you're in front of a room interacting with people, with a clear idea of where you want to take them, you will likely know what to say. (I do know this takes practice, and even those who have the skills don't step right into using them off the bat; this is why we practice skills all the time in my programs!) With your intuition and your affection for your programs, you can easily stretch what might seem like minimal content into a successful retreat.

A retreat I did for three years was called the Inner Alignment Intensive, and the entire retreat grew from three sentences or concepts – I like to call them conversations – and one experiential assignment. The rest of the two-and-a-half days was organic. The huge benefit of this approach was that it allowed plenty of space for what came up. With that type of open agenda you can address people right where they are and allow for the conversation that *really* needs to unfold. If you have too much rigid content, you aren't going to have the time or energy to meet people where they are and guide their awakening.

Content is king... sort of. Often less is more. When you condense what you do into a four-to-six-room castle floor, you have enough of a model to be golden!

EXERCISE:

The Rooms in Your Castle

Take the steps you mapped out for your three clients and turn them into rooms in your castle. Ideally you'll have four to six rooms. They represent the work that your clients need to do in order to get to the destination.

Give each room a name. Ideally the names of the rooms kind of flow together nicely, such as "Own It, Offer It, Amplify It, Elevate It," or "Story, Success, Stepping out, Systematize," or "Power, Passion, Purpose, Play, Profit." Or maybe an acronym like I use in my HEART formula for positioning your offer – Hallway, Experience, Audience, Reality, Trust (more about that in chapter 11). It's okay if they don't fit together so nicely, but it's worth some time to give it a shot! Steps that are easy to remember make it easier for your clients to apply what they learn and know what they need from you next!

Now you've mapped your content so you will be able to choose what goes where in your business model/castle. Great job!

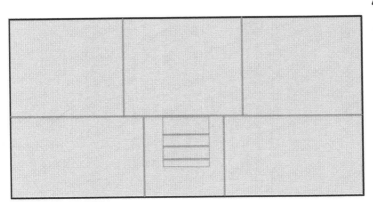

purpose
insight
attract/pull
intuit
passion
action
accountability

purp
insight
passion
how
action

purpose
passion
pull
play

purpose
passion
attraction
action
accountabilty

Your next step in the process of reverse-engineering your programs in order to design the ideal RR is to develop your awesome HLP. We'll do this in the next chapter.

Chapter 7

Your High-Level Program — Support Comes in Containers

Leann was tired. She'd been in business five years working with clients one on one as their business and life coach. She didn't really love talking about business, but she loved inspiring women to take their power back. Her clients made miraculous changes in their lives by deciding to put themselves first, do the things that felt scary, and make lasting changes in their lives.

I'd known Leann for several years when she asked me for help. Things just weren't working and she knew she needed to make a shift. When she looked at her calendar for the upcoming week and saw all of her clients scheduled, she had this negative gut reaction that she didn't want to admit. As much as she loved certain aspects of her work — like butt-kicking her clients into action and reminding them of their power — she did not love having regular calls with them. She'd been doing these for so long that they'd become boring. Many of her clients wanted to solve practical business challenges, and that wasn't what she really wanted to talk about. She wanted to address their relationships with themselves; she wanted to help them tap in to their own decision-making compasses; she wanted to help them think differently and live passionate, turned-on lives.

But making a change was scary for her. She'd established herself as a premium provider of business coaching services. She'd been making great money. She'd moved to a home that she wouldn't be able to afford if her new plan didn't work.

She also had all kinds of beliefs about why people hired her that weren't really true. She thought she had to do one-on-one coaching because that was what they needed, and she thought she needed to be a business coach because that was the only thing that people would pay for.

Yet she was committed to changing her business. She knew she had a purpose on the planet and she wanted to do work that would truly light her soul on fire! She had been there before and she wanted that again. Leann needed to shift her thinking. She needed to stop focusing on what she saw other people doing in her industry. She needed to look at the value she could deliver in a different way. While she was charging a premium and making good money, she was still essentially trading hours for dollars. She felt that the value was in her time rather than in her knowledge, energy, inspiration, and the container she had designed.

Leann had to let this go and consider what she believed delivered the most value to her clients and why, and how she wanted to design her life. When did she want to work? *How* did she want to work? Which parts of her work lit her up and which parts were draining or unenjoyable?

She knew that the power of the live experience was palpable for her clients. She loved hosting live retreats and events and being in the front of the room. And for Leann, the bigger the room the better – she pictured herself with a large community of powerhouse women lifting each other up and connecting. All her intuition, as well as her Human Design (a tool I suggest all my clients use for self-understanding, which I cover in chapter 9), pointed to her being meant to work through community.

She enjoyed teaching concepts and answering questions. She usually knew just what to say without much planning. And she loved "text coaching." While she hated scheduled phone calls and hated emails, she absolutely delighted in being able to text someone the right message at the right time. And she enjoyed texting in her life in general.

First we tentatively crafted a program, or a "container of support," based only on these things she loved and believed. She included live events, training, group Q&A calls, a Facebook forum to connect with the community, weekly text challenges, and access to her for coaching via text.

She got really clear about what would happen at the live events, how people would flow through her curriculum, and what the outcome would be: becoming fully present, turned on, empowered, and totally sensual. Her clients would have more of what they wanted in their lives as a result of this shift. And the things they wanted were healthy, happy relationships, looking and feeling great, and financial success.

In this new container there would not be a focus on talking about business marketing strategies, which she didn't enjoy. Because she pictured herself with a large community of women, she would remove her one-on-one scheduled calls from her program, divert her focus away from business coaching, and still be able to make the same amount of money by designing a carefully crafted container of support. She would double the number of clients she worked with and cut the investment for the program in half from what she was charging for private coaching. These changes would mean that she could actually continue to add more clients and revenue if she wanted to grow. She'd have no scheduled one-on-one calls on her calendar, she'd be working in a way that lit her up, and she'd be making the money she made before, or more!

Next we went through her list of favorite clients one by one and asked, "Would Mary be best served in a one-on-one program or in this new program?" "Would Samantha be best served in a one-on-one program or in this new program?" She discovered that the new program would be better for all of her favorite clients. She felt she was actually holding them back from the most efficient and effective result by clinging to the way she thought she had to do things! Her new offering would reach more people, better serve them at a soul level, and let her work at her very best! Win, win, win!

Support Comes in Containers

I like to think of your top-notch solution for your clients not as a program or an offering or a package, but as a *container of support*. Through the way you choose to design your offering you are setting up the structure for the container and giving your clients a place to play and grow.

In this chapter you will design your High-Level Program (your high-level container of support). Before you do this, I want to help you understand the "why" behind developing this container. Your three core programs are distinct containers of support that deliver specific outcomes. Your HLP is the container of support that takes them all the way. It includes everything that is in your Gateway and your RR, and goes deep into the rest of the rooms in your castle as well. Your HLP is offered to graduates of your RR. Roughly half of your retreat participants will join you in your HLP. These are your STAR clients, and you want to design your HLP for them.

Why is it helpful to think of your programs as containers? When people are choosing to work with you to get a result, while it is true that some quickly calculate your hourly rate, most are focused on the outcome they will get. If you can get them a result with less effort, all the better; let go of the idea that you are charging for your time. You are providing the outcome they desire – a transformation from being in pain at the bus stop to enjoying the benefits at the destination.

You will design a container of support that includes all the practical and energetic pieces that guide your client to the destination. You will use your personal expertise to create value by deciding what goes in it. You will decide how long the container lasts and thereby set the intention for the outcome to be accomplished in a particular time period. When I use the word *intention* I'm talking about being clear as to what you and your client, together, intend to bring about during the time frame. This is both a literal intention that guides you to behave in a certain way, and an energetic intention through which you invite Spirit or the Universe in general to support you in achieving the outcome.

You will provide the outline or the boundaries of the container in terms of how your client accesses support from you during this time period. You will co-create the intention for the container based on how you talk about it in your marketing. You will provide tools and information for navigating the container in the form of sharing content (approaches, information, checklists, systems, inspiration, etc.). You will paint a clear picture of what life is like at the destination. But most of all you will be an undauntable energetic force for accessing that destination. In other words, you will hold the energetic space for your client to create a new outcome in their life, health, business, or relationships. When they are tempted to go back to approaching their issue the old way, you will be there to remind them of what they said they really want. You cannot do it for them, but your energetic stand can make a big difference.

And here's what's super cool about containers: You define the container, your client agrees to the container and buys in with a commitment to the outcomes, and it's as if you just formed an energetic contract with Spirit to help guide the outcome for both of you! You declare, "Hey Spirit, we'd like to get to *here* by *this time*," thereby opening up the channel for that to happen. A high-level container of support is often called a *mastermind*, because the joining of the two minds and the inclusion of Spirit forms a master-mind.

I like to include group components in HLPs (group phone calls and live retreats) so that each client benefits from the practical and energetic work done by the other clients in that same program. When we purchase individual sessions with a service provider, or even packages of sessions, but they are not designed as a container of support with clear start and end times, clearly defined outcomes, and a holistic view of what the support looks like, we do not get the same level of results.

I fell on some stairs and hurt myself earlier this year. Turns out I dislocated my shoulder. It took seven different medical professionals/practitioners to help me figure that out. No one offered me a *container of support* to help me solve my problem and heal fully. Initially I ignored the injury, assuming it would heal. Then I realized that it wasn't going to heal on its own, that I had spent months compensating for the injury and causing other physical issues and patterns, and that it was probably going to take an effort on my part to release those patterns.

I was aware that there was an emotional component (I am a firm believer in the mind-body code) and a very real physical component. I longed to find someone who would offer me holistic expertise, and was ready and willing to pay the right person (or people) to support me through the healing journey. No one offered me this type of solution. I bought a five-session massage package at a local spa. I did many one-off sessions in acupuncture and physical therapy, several at traditional doctors, and several approaches to bodywork and integrated therapies. I sometimes received recommendations for what I could do on my own that "might help." The acupuncturist did the best job in that she always asked me to schedule my next session before I left, which I did. Yet each time I went back she didn't remember what my injury was or ask whether the work was helping, and she didn't provide me with any resources that could have helped my cause.

One person told me that the exercises my doctor had recommended were not going to help and would probably even hurt, thus discouraging me from doing the one thing I had been doing consistently. Because this was the person who had put my shoulder back into place and had helped me the most, I did not take his advice lightly.

I discontinued the whole process. I am absolutely certain that in the big, progressive, metropolitan area of Seattle where I live there is a holistic practitioner who could have provided a well-rounded solution, but my Google searches came up empty.

What about a solution that addressed the emotional *and* physical; that included treatment, education, and homework I could do between sessions; that would support me in asking for help when I was stuck or in pain; that would provide accountability for my progress; that would provide connection to a community of others on similar healing journeys? I invested a fair amount of money in random sessions, the bulk of which had zero impact. If I could have invested all of that with one person and known I was in a healing *container of support*, it would have saved me loads of tears, anxiety, internet research, driving around town, and wondering if I would ever be whole again. That container would have been worth a lot!

I believe that some of the people I purchased time with actually had the tools to help me heal, but they had likely never thought about their work in terms of a container. They had likely not stopped to consider how they could engage my intention for healing with their skillset into a time-based structure to support me in reaching my goal. They also likely had never covered what we did earlier in the book about money and value and asking and receiving.

For inquiring minds who want to know, the shoulder injury (shouldering responsibility) caused me to simplify several things in my life and my business and led to the writing of this book. Writing had been something I longed to do once everything else was handled! At this moment, at my computer, I still experience shoulder pain, though I'm almost fully mobile and back to working out and feeling confident that full recovery is in sight!

I know I got loads of juice out of the emotional message of not being able to find an ideal partner for my recovery from that injury. I wonder if perhaps I didn't find the right person in the right way so that I could rant here in this chapter about the necessity of containers!

Retreat Revenue Revolution

Even if you have never hosted a retreat, create a high-level container of support that your clients can invest in at a level that forces them to take your work seriously. I'm not saying that everyone must want a multiple-six- or seven-figure business, or even that everyone must do retreats; but invite your clients to work with you at a level that gives them a surefire opportunity to reach their solution and feel supported along the way.

Our world is so fast-paced, and getting faster every minute. On a typical day I have an average of nineteen windows open on my laptop – some are tasks I'm in the middle of, others are reminders of things to do later, and some are distractions from work (cute puppies anyone?). I've read the books about focus and multitasking and all that jazz, and sometimes I follow their advice; I'm working on improving those habits. But I am a busy human being with lots of priorities tugging at me at all times, and making something happen just because I want it to can be a herculean feat, especially when it requires a significant change of habits and patterns or implementing new knowledge and awareness, as all transformational shifts require.

Day after day we attempt to face these tasks alone. Perhaps you want to lose weight by changing your eating habits, but you live in a household full of pasta and cheese, so you have to try to do it on your own. Perhaps you want to double the profitability of your business, but you really have no idea how to do things differently, so you have to try to find out how to do it on your own. Perhaps you want to change the way you earn money, but the way you've been doing it is so predictable that you're afraid to make the change, so you try to change just a little bit and then quit because it doesn't work. When you do such a thing on your own, all you can see is that the little bit didn't work, whereas someone with a slightly different perspective might be able to see that you are just three feet from gold.

We live in a world in which doing it alone is a badge of honor, and I've had enough of it. We are meant to live and work in community. We are meant to be great at the things we're great at and to allow others to be great at the things they are great at, as families and tribes throughout history have done for eons. With the advent of money and the cultural focus on earning money to survive, we've shifted to spending all our time working (often at a job we don't like and are not particularly good at), and we have no time or space for supporting one another. We've grown more and more disconnected, and as I mentioned earlier, this has created loads of problems for society.

I'm passionate about retreats because they allow us to create connection as we achieve our goals rather than remain siloed, disconnected, and struggling. Through this live experience of finding a clear path to your solution, you can wrap your mind around why we need support and community to stay committed to our paths.

The changes you want to make often don't stick because the people around you don't want you to change and your physical environment doesn't support your change. If you want a life of abundance yet are constantly surrounded by reminders of scarcity, especially in conversations with people in your environment, it is very hard to create the abundance you desire. When you know that the secret to life is to love yourself (it is, by the way), but those around you don't support self-love and judge you as selfish, you quickly slip into feeling like they might be right. I could go on and on with examples of this, but I know you're picking up what I'm laying down. ENVIRONMENT is the number-one contributor to success. That's why it's critical to provide a *container* for people to get into a new habitat and explore what they really want to create. And this is why providing an opportunity for that new environment is something I just can't say enough about.

I am a perfectly smart, capable, educated, and highly committed person. I would have never... I repeat, *never* created my business on my own in the spare bedroom of my house in Cincinnati, Ohio. I would not have changed my life such that I found the perfect marriage, and been able to accept it, had I not hired mentors to support my growth. I would not have healed myself from back pain in my early thirties without a program that helped me become more aware of the emotional causes of my pain. I would not have lost thirty pounds and permanently shifted my relationship to food without a container of support for that transformation. And I would not have finished this book without a coach and a structure for support to make it happen. I repeat, I am *not* the kind of person who doesn't get things done on my own; but left to my own devices I will spend too much time getting the wrong things done or thinking repetitive thoughts I'm not even aware of that will not take me toward my goal.

When I'm connecting with someone or experiencing a high-vibration collective energy, I tune in with the thoughts that are in harmony with where I truly want to go, and life becomes easy.

I hope we live to see a day when we don't need to create containers for this type of transformation because the world is just vibrating on its own at a high level of joy. Today it's not, and I believe we owe it to ourselves and one another to get the support we need to bring us our joy.

You can look at the current lack of support in our environment and say, "What a shame that we have to *pay* for support to make change and get things done!" I remember David Letterman once said of life coaches, "Didn't we used to call them friends?" As a burgeoning life coach you can imagine I didn't find that very funny. It is sad that our friends often don't have time to support us in our goals. With rare exceptions (I am grateful to have found some of these exceptions) our friends are more committed to our staying the same than they are to our growth. It's not because they want us to stay small (though sometimes they do), but rather it's just human nature. As humans we like to remain in control of as much as possible so we can minimize our risk, know what to expect, play the game of life, and survive. Your friends and family are actually very invested in your staying who you are, because they know what they can expect from you, what you'll show up for and what you won't, how you'll respond, and what you'll wear. They know whether or not they can count on you not to embarrass them, not to look cuter than them, and to always be the life of the party. The moment you change, it threatens their perception of their own survival.

Think about your dowdiest friend who you know you can wear your yoga pants next to and still look great by comparison. Now imagine her becoming a radiant diva who is always dressed to the nines, turning heads everywhere you go. Well shit, you just might have to put clothes on to hang out with her now, right? So why would you want to encourage that kind of transformation? (Okay, you likely would if she took the time to talk to you about it and get you invested in who she wants to become, but that's the advanced class.) This newly transformed friend might express interest in dressing up to go dancing, flirting with the idea of changing her persona, and you might conveniently be unavailable that night or talk her into a movie instead (your ego can feel the impending shift and gets scared). She had a moment of inspiration, but because it's not supported, she doesn't take action and the moment fades. Back to dowdy she goes.

Now imagine this friend finds herself in a sensual empowerment retreat where she gets really tuned in to her second chakra and lit up by the idea of showing off her curves. (Who knew she had such a killer body under those bulky sweaters?) On a whim, during one of the breaks, she purchases the red dress that's to die for. She wears it the next day and those who don't have years of background history with her go wild. She feels different and people treat her differently and she really likes it. The retreat comes to an end and she heads back home and puts this rockin' red dress in her closet. But there's nowhere to wear it, no one who gets that that is who she is now, and she's terrified to bust it out again! And there the dress sits — a memory of that time when she expressed that other side of herself that she loves.

But, wait! Imagine that the retreat leader had offered her a six-month container of support (HLP) to continue her journey of sensual empowerment! Imagine that she had two more retreats ahead of her with many of the same women and she already knows she'll get to wear that dress again, or maybe even buy another. She'd be given assignments and opportunities to express this new side of herself over six months. She'd get support for navigating her current relationships as she becomes more of who she truly is. She'd have the chance to redefine how she relates to herself and get comfortable changing her environment (and her wardrobe) to reflect this. WOW! What a gift!

Many retreat leaders think they should somehow be able to deliver all the transformation during their retreat, and this is just not possible. A lot of tangible change can happen in a single retreat, and for the person with a completely supportive environment, this may be enough. But most people need further support. They will gratefully pay you for creating a container, which comes easily and naturally to you but is a total value shift and realignment for them in the context of their world. This is the "retreat revenue revolution." They pay you, then they pay you again, and they feel completely generous in the process!

Now I want to touch the money thing one more time. As Letterman said, we used to call life coaches friends. We've established that our friends often unknowingly hold us back through their commitments to safety, security, and wanting us to be predictable, even in little ways. The expectation that we stay the same has a powerful effect on us, well beyond what we wear. Our friends buy in to our stories about why we can't change, they are on our sides when we feel victimized by the world, and they are very eager to treat us as if we can't change. So, no, Mr. Letterman, our friends are not our life coaches.

But you still might be tempted to ask the question, "But should I really pay someone to help me wear a red dress (or eat healthier food, or make sales calls)? *Really?* Shouldn't I be able to do it on my own?" This is buying in to the societal myth of the superhero.

Back in the time before money, we essentially bartered our services. Someone was the tribe's storyteller, someone else was the tribe's housekeeper, someone else was the wood collector, and another the doctor. You might get to sit by the fire you made, enjoy the heat, and eat the food someone else caught for the group, and maybe it's my job to tell you stories; we shared our energy. At some point we invented money because we wanted to barter with people who weren't in our immediate tribe. Now we exchange goods and services with people all over the world. Money *represents* that shared *energy*. Take note of this: Money is energy.

We decided as a culture that it's okay to pay money for certain things like TVs and running shoes, especially if they come through a big company that employs a lot of people. We also think it's okay to pay for services from professionals like doctors and lawyers. And then there are things that we decided we *shouldn't* pay for, like education, therapy, and human connection.

We make cultural agreements to pay for things that come from big corporations, many of which are actively harming our environment and overworking their employees, and not to pay for services from our friends and neighbors who put their hearts on the line to do their best work in the world. And I personally take issue with these choices.

We *can* create our own economy. We *can* choose to pay for things we truly value, and choose not to pay for things that aren't important or beneficial to us. And we can support others in earning a living doing what they love.

An investment in transformational work that shifts your beliefs about yourself and others and moves you toward the energy of unconditional self-love is likely an investment that will save you a whole lot of money in other areas. You can save on "retail therapy." You can save on health care because you've worked yourself to wellness. You can save on changing jobs again because you've found a career you love. So let's start a revolution, shall we?

Reverse-Engineering Your Container

In the previous chapter you determined the number and content of the rooms in your castle. In your HLP, or container of support, your clients get an all-access pass to this second floor of your castle. You are going to give them all of what they need to move from pain to destination as efficiently as possible. They get each room, in the order that works best for you and for them, and they might even have access to bonus rooms on the third floor that you don't even talk about in your marketing.

My high-level clients get to work with me to develop each of the pieces of their multiple-six-figure retreat-based businesses. They also get the experiences I create at each retreat, from self-expression in the parade on the streets of New Orleans to making the leap at a zip-line in Oregon. The shifts that happen in these bonding experiences are unique to each client and beyond description. I am also an open book with my high-level clients. I share what I do in my business so they get information and an intimate connection with someone who is most often ten steps ahead of them. I introduce them to my personal resources and rolodexes and share my tools with them as they develop.

This is always how I've done business. It may or may not suit you in your business, but it's a great fit for my personality. I like to know I'm being paid well to work with clients who are committed, and I like to be generous. I also learn from my clients about what works best, and share that generously in lower-priced packaged offerings (or retreats) geared to broader audiences that have less access to the rest of the castle.

Designing Your HLP — What Goes in the Container?

The first HLP I ever created, the Sweet Spot Inner Circle, included a few specific items that created the boundaries for the container: The HLP was six months. My clients and I aligned ourselves with the idea that they would get a specific outcome in those six months, in this case redesigning their businesses such that they were operating smack in the center of their business sweet spots. I included two one-on-one sessions and two group masterminding sessions each month.

In the group sessions I taught a short lesson each time (~twenty minutes) on a topic that I intuitively felt would resonate or speak to a need that the collective group had at that time. (I was pretty tapped in to this based on having had one-on-one calls with them.) I would then open up the line for Q&A. This was a chance for them to connect to the group and recognize that they were not alone in their journeys.

I also included two live two-and-a-half-day retreats during the six months so we could come together in person and work on their mindsets and their marketing.

There was a group forum (Facebook group), email support (these days I give email support very selectively), and a monthly as-needed "clearing call" – a short call to get them back on track if they felt they were off. These elements assured them of a place to go to stay on track, either with me or with the group, if they bumped up against resistance in executing their plans.

Access to the right information or the right energetic perspective, at the right time, is priceless. That's what you want to design into your container. No information is totally unique; it's out there on the Internet. What isn't readily available is someone who has sifted through it to find the right information and is there when their clients need it. When your clients are in the midst of transformation they often don't know what they need in that moment, nor do they have the time to find it. You are ready for that. Your work in deciding what's included in your container – and just as important, *what's not* – is juicy and exciting.

What's Not in Your Container?

Choosing what doesn't go in your container is almost as important as choosing what does. You want clear boundaries about what happens in the rooms of your castle. Then think about what other support they might need, and what you are *not* going to cover. When I hired my new bookkeeper and accounting team, they clearly told me that payroll services and paying my estimated taxes would not be included in their work. Sure, they could do that, but they prefer to focus on what they do best. I help people get clear about what and how to market, but I don't do their marketing for them. A weight-loss coach might provide guidelines on what to eat, but not provide recipes because they believe that if you choose your recipes you'll be more likely to stick with them; another who embraces their unique gift for making shopping lists might provide recipes if they love being more prescriptive about what to eat.

There is no right or wrong in terms of what goes in your castle and container. What is important is that it is your truth and that you don't add things that are outside of your genius because you think they make the container sound better or more valuable. Anything you are not absolutely awesome at deserves a referral to someone who loves doing it. When you are skillful at marketing your genius you can add team members to do the other things and expand your offerings if you want to, but this isn't the direction in which most of you will choose to go.

Container Building Blocks

These building blocks ADD VALUE to your program without adding much (or any) workload for you. Randomly including more things doesn't always create more value. I've done this myself, adding features to my program that seemed great, but combined with everything else, led to overwhelm. A streamlined and efficient program is the goal.

Below are some examples of what to include in your HLP. Remember to first define the length of your program (how long you think it will take them to get to the destination), then choose the features that will help them get there. Start with no more than three to five features.

- Regular one-on-one sessions with you — from one to four per month

- Special one-on-one sessions with you, such as a kick-off or intention-setting call, an assessment and debrief session, and pivot-point sessions at particular points in the journey when a longer session is needed

- Group calls led by you using a system like Instant Teleseminar, Skype, Zoom, Go To Meeting, etc. These can be designed as teaching or content calls, laser-coaching or mastermind calls, or a combination (my favorite).

- Guest expert training sessions or interviews. You might not be the top expert in all the things that are important in getting to the outcome, so bring in outside experts to add to the container! They can support and validate your perspective or add an additional skill above and beyond your work.

- Live retreats, of course! Include one to three live, two- to four-day retreats. (They can be longer if there is a specific reason for it.) These can be training or content retreats centered around a specific theme, or pure mastermind retreats where each person has a chance to get their burning issue addressed in front of the room. Retreats that are included with your High-Level Program are called *fulfillment* retreats, and are especially valuable because of their exclusivity.

- Special virtual group sessions. You can choose to do a virtual training via livestream or even a virtual mastermind day. I like to hold "implementation days" (I call them "Simplementation Days"): we start the day together, establish a specific project to be done, check in part way through, and then end the day together, having worked individually or in groups to get our projects completed!

- Training or courses. Record your information so that each client from now into infinity can benefit from it but you only teach it once. This can be regularly released curriculum that you preplan and define, or spontaneous lessons that you intuit and share. You might record tools like guided meditations via audio or video. If you already have loads of this, set it up as a content library so clients can access it at any time. Or you might have one specific training course that guides all of your work, supplemented by coaching – and that works too.

- Checklists, templates, and tip-sheets. Even if you teach this material in your sessions or training, providing a template or checklist to guide your clients each time they do it is super helpful.

- Your process made tangible. If you teach something that is foundational to creating results, make it a big deal and take the time to craft it as a guiding process for clients in a usable format such as a morning ritual, a specific meditation set, an intention-setting guide, a numerology toolkit, etc.

- Access to other clients through a group format on Facebook, Google Groups, etc.

- Accountability structures. Create a structure for accountability outside of your individual support, such as a weekly accountability form, a place where they can check off completed coursework, a weekly Facebook check-in system, accountability groups, or "gamifying" the results of the program for public accountability.

- VIP Days. These are blocks of time, full or half days, spent with you in person (though they can also be conducted via Skype). The longer block of time allows clients to unpack their issues, shift their thinking, and craft complete solutions.

- Feedback. If appropriate to your work, add in a structured way to provide feedback on your clients' work. I review clients' recorded sales calls, webinars, and video scripts and read their marketing campaign copy two to three times per year to give them specific, directional feedback. For example, if you are a personal stylist you might audit your clients' closets. If you are a book coach you might read a certain number of pages each week or month. If you are a health coach you might check on your clients' pantries, in person or via video call.

- Done-for-them projects. Depending on the work you do, you can execute some of your clients' projects for them, like writing, creative work, project work, etc. At various points in my tenure I have written marketing copy for clients who struggled with it, for a price or thrown in as a bonus.

- Promotion. You can do mailings to your subscriber list for your clients or promote them on social media as part of their work with you. Use this offer strategically, as it has great value for the right person and little value for others; it must be lined up with the outcome intended.

- A book club or study group, and send them the book. This can be a great add-on to create unity among your tribe and promote a specific outcome.
- A custom-created workbook or journal to guide your clients' process.
- Gifts that support the journey.

Phew! As you can see, that is quite a list! There is no shortage of ways to shape your program to create value for your clients. Remember, streamlined and efficient is better than too many features they won't know how to use! I hope this list excites you as you think about what's possible! Don't forget that you can use technology to strategically deliver the right information at the right time without even tracking or managing it! It's okay to do it manually in the beginning; just do your thing!

Features versus Benefits

The above lists FEATURES of your HLP – the specific details of what's included in your program. Depending on how savvy your clients are, they actually don't care that much about the features! (I know, you just spent all this time reading about features and now I tell you they don't even care!) What they do care about are the BENEFITS – what they get to be, do, or have in their lives when they get to the destination, such as more free time to do the things they love, being a great role model for their children, more money in their checking account at the end of each month, or deeper connection with their romantic partner and better sex! The latter are *benefits*. You listed three to five of them in the previous chapter.

The *features* you carefully design into your program are the actions your clients take inside your castle. The features are designed to give them the best experience once they get there so that they want to stay and tell all their friends about it. But for the most part they don't need to know what the features are in order to get on your bus and cross your drawbridge; they just want to know who they will be when they leave the castle on the other side. While you want to define the features and share what they are once your client commits to working with you, focus on the benefits rather than the features.

There are two exceptions to this approach. Exception one is when an especially savvy prospective client wants to know how much access they will have to you. More access usually means a firmer container of support, and usually, though not always, correlates to a larger price tag. Exception two is when a particular feature really positions you well in their minds. For example, if you are an astrologist and you use someone's chart to guide your work, you will likely want to talk about that with your potential clients to attract believers in that approach – the chart work is both a benefit *and* a feature.

Pricing Your HLP

I actually use a different pricing approach for each program in the Retreat and Grow Rich Business System. When pricing your HLP I recommend "Desire-Based Pricing."

Desire-Based Pricing is just as it sounds. It is using your personal desires to guide the investment you receive for your program. I believe that desire is of Spirit (de-sire = of the father). I believe that true desires are your most authentic guides for your own growth and direction. A desire doesn't come to you by accident; it is actually for your growth. Most of us learned to tune out our desires at an early age, and therefore experience self-doubt when it comes to our desires. "Am I too much?" "Is that selfish?" "I don't need much!" etc. Or, on the other end, "If I make a million dollars I will be abundant and I won't need to think about money."

None of these create an environment for accurately tuning in to your desire. But your real desires are brilliant guides. To price your HLP, identify two core desires:

1) What is the LIFESTYLE I desire (and what will it cost?)
2) How many high-level clients do I desire?

To understand the lifestyle you desire, I recommend looking at the cost of the lifestyle you have now and adding in the additional handful of things you'd truly like NOW that would noticeably change your level of fulfillment or quality of life. My clients often select a couple of lifestyle upgrades like a larger home or an annual overseas vacation.

In addition, you'll want to add in a budget for running your business. This includes paying for systems that can automate things for you, team and coaching support, and travel to wonderful retreat places as a business expense. For most people with a multiple-six-figure business goal, a rule of thumb is that you will take home roughly half of your revenue, with the other half being used to run the business.

How many high-level clients you desire can be harder to determine if you haven't worked in this way before. In the beginning take your best guess.

Most of my clients desire somewhere between eight and sixteen high-level clients. I have some who see themselves building a larger community, in which case they start with a number like thirty or fifty. Start with a smaller number to price the initial program such that you have more revenue and more time to work with as you build your bigger community.

To calculate your pricing, you simply divide the dollar amount needed to fund your desired lifestyle on a monthly basis by the number of clients you desire in your HLP at any given time. As an example, let's say that Chris has been living on $6,000/month take home. He would like to sustain his current lifestyle, move to a nicer apartment, and take his girlfriend on a luxury vacation twice a year. He determines he can do this with $10,000/month. He also wants to do less of the day-to-day operations of his business, so wants to hire a team member or two and set up some systems online. He's also going to be hosting retreats, so traveling more for his business. Using the rule of thumb, he decides his revenue goals should be $20,000/month.

Having worked with clients before in a different business, Chris knows that his capacity for individual work is twelve clients.

His High-Level Program will thus be a monthly investment of $20,000/12 = $1,667. He likes to work with clients in six-month increments, so the average investment for a client for six months is $1,667 x 6 = $10,000.

What is your Desire-Based Pricing? What is your reaction to this idea? If you think about it, this is a much more aligned approach to pricing than many others. Most people randomly research six other people doing what they do and use that to set their pricing – only they know nothing about those six people and how they "do what they do."

You might notice that your Desire-Based Pricing doesn't take into account your other programs. YES, this is absolutely true! This approach sets you up to earn the money that you need in your one core program and leaves space for your RICH Retreat not to have to make money up front. It also means that your Gateway Program will create bonus money that will help fund your growth. More of this as we go.

After you decide on the price for your HLP, you can ask yourself, "How do I deliver and exceed that level of value with my programs?" You'll be surprised how fun and fulfilling this work is! And one way to do it is to create community in your absolutely amazing, client-exclusive live retreats!

EXERCISE:

Craft Your High-Level Program

Get out a clean sheet of paper or a giant flip chart to capture your big ideas. Using the list above as inspiration, decide what features to include in your container of support.

Now that you've defined your HLP, you have a clear sense of how you will ultimately work with your STAR clients. The time is right to now craft your RICH Retreat!

Chapter 8

Your RICH Retreat, Part I –
Castle Tour or House Party?

I was staring at my email. Refresh. Refresh. I'd just launched my first online coaching program, Decide Then Thrive, and I was waiting for the orders to come in. I'd done everything I saw everyone else doing online, so I was ready for the money to just start rolling in.

I had a small list I'd generated from the Freedom Summit I'd hosted a few months earlier, and I figured this was the next step. It was a six-month mastermind program that I knew would change people's lives. I visualized myself launching the program and seeing the avalanche of orders!

Refresh. Refresh. No orders yet. I'd spent a good two months preparing for this program. I had a logo designed. I painstakingly wrote a web page about it. I carefully crafted my email launch. Mind you, my business coach had advised me not to go this route, but I had this superiorly awesome online program in my mind and I couldn't shake it. I was subscribed to at least twenty-one newsletters from other coaches and had watched them send their newsletters, offer their programs, and by the third week the program would say "Sold Out!" I did the math about how much money they were making by *sending emails*, and I decided I wanted some of that.

Refresh again. Crickets. Zero sales. Zero interest in Decide Then Thrive. I know, I know – who really feels excited to decide then thrive? I can see now it wasn't the best name! "Thrive" alone would have been better. I was so set on clients understanding my amazing process and insight that I wasn't really thinking about them and what they wanted.

But it wasn't the name that mattered. What mattered was that my strategy wasn't sound. These people didn't know me. They had no idea how amazingly awesome I would be at helping them make clear and empowered decisions that would move them forward. How could they? I'd just sent them a couple of emails! Aside from my fabulous newsletter articles, I hadn't done any education-based marketing to help them get to know me or to deliver value.

As much as I loved providing value, I really didn't know what to give. I didn't know enough about my audience to speak their language. I was stuck in my own head trying to think of how to express everything awesome about me into the name of my program. And while I knew I needed to make it about my clients, I really didn't know how. I'd only been in business six months and I was newly exposed to the world of entrepreneurial coaching circles. I didn't know the lingo or the pain or the desires of this audience. I didn't know my clients at all. I was still new and ambitious and optimistic, so I didn't know the pain of someone who wasn't. I needed to learn. First I needed to let go of that program!

One of the top benefits of hosting retreats, which I stumbled upon unintentionally, is earning while you learn. And learn I did. One of the things I quickly came to understand was that in 2009 there were a lot of untruths out there in Internet marketing. When some people wrote "Sold Out" on their program, what it really meant was that they didn't sell anything and they were going to give up and save face by calling it sold out. I also learned that a successful online launch required larger numbers of followers than I had, and a much bigger marketing effort, including layers of education. I had 500 people on my list. Filling an online program through email marketing takes more people than that and more effort than I had invested. The percentage of people who take each action is quite small. I didn't know that then.

In the wake of my defeat I had to pause and take stock. What did I really want to be doing? How did I want to spend my time? How could I deliver value to the people who needed it most? An idea began to form....

When I had dreamed about becoming a coach, 100 percent of the time I pictured myself leading a small group of people on a transformational journey. My visions were always in the form of workshops or small retreats. Then I was introduced to the world of online marketing and set that vision aside in favor of what I thought I was supposed to do. When I remembered my vision again after my online marketing disappointment, I decided to revive my dream and host my first retreat. I'd been to a few of them and had liked the live experience. I'd also watched event hosts make offers for coaching programs. I myself signed on with my first business mentor through an event like that. Why couldn't I do something similar?

I did a little asking around to get advice about booking a venue, and I went for it. I booked my first event at an Embassy Suites hotel in Nashville, Tennessee. I'd learned that it was important for people to get of their home environments to truly immerse themselves in transformation, and that there must be a major airport nearby. I offered my existing clients the opportunity to attend the retreat for free. I raffled off free tickets at local networking events and sold the remaining seats in one-on-one conversations with people I met locally at $297 each. I also did some light marketing for free consultations to those on my email list. The expenses at the Embassy were pretty low, and that hotel chain offers free breakfast.

I was nervous as hell and had fear every step of the way. I didn't know if the things I had planned would work the way I imagined them. I had spoken to each of my attendees personally, so I had an intuitive sense of what each of them needed. I had designed elements to "drive up their emotional shit" so they could also access what they really needed.

I love games at retreats, so when the attendees arrived at the hotel they received a gift bag with some snacks, a note, an agenda, and an invitation to play a game. The assignment involved connecting with as many people as possible before we started the next day at 9:00 a.m. I suggested specific types of people to find and connect with, sort of like a scavenger hunt but with people. The next morning we would debrief the game, score everyone, and award a prize to the winner. This game was the crux of the teaching for the first day, allowing us to dive right in to how they played the game and how the way they played the game related to what was going on for them in their businesses.

I'd never done this before. I believed it would work… but I didn't really know. I was running on faith.

And it worked better than I imagined. By the end of the first day several people had "popped" (my word for what happens when someone sees and embraces a whole new truth about themselves right before your eyes!). We had started talking truth and getting to the bottom of what really mattered for each of the people in the room. It was awesome!

I had planned to make an offer for my High-Level Program at the retreat. I had my order forms printed. I was excited about my program. It was a significantly higher investment than any of my clients in the room had ever paid me. The morning of the offer I prayed as I was getting ready in my presidential suite. (I'd gotten an upgrade for hosting, and I knew I could get used to that presidential treatment!) I can still see myself clear as day standing outside that conference room in Nashville after lunch, pausing, looking up, and asking Spirit, "Please, may the greatest and highest good unfold here today." I was 100 percent running on faith.

As you know, it worked out well for me. Leaving for home with order forms for $36,000 in coaching was a surreal experience. That was as much money as I had originally imagined *eventually* making in a *year*! And here it was in my hands on those pieces of paper. I was thrilled. And I told no one in my life about what had just happened.

I thought others would judge me. (I'm pretty sure I was right about that.) I was still in shock that I could make money doing what I loved, what came naturally, and what I believed in. Thankfully I was a participant in my own business mastermind through which I could share my success and make it feel real!

Here's the absolute best part of the story: I learned. I learned so much in that weekend of speaking truth with those participants. I learned what they really thought, what they really feared, what was really getting in the way, and the desires they had deep down. This made me a better marketer.

Over the following six months I learned even more. After adding two more people to the program from my email list, I had eight ideal clients I was able to learn from for the next six months while I paid my bills with money I had earned coaching! By using what I learned from these people I became more effective at marketing to my email list. Over the coming months my client base shifted from 80 percent local to 80 percent online, and before I knew it I was location independent.

Following my heart about what I wanted to do guided me to discovering the best approach to growing my business, and hopefully it will guide you to expanding your business as well. This approach allows you to earn while you learn and master your marketing message without going broke trying a bunch of stuff that's not for you.

The Fastest Way to Grow You and Your Clients!

Hosting your retreat is the fastest way to grow both *you* and your clients! I am a huge fan of creating a business in which you can EARN while you LEARN. Most people keep waiting until they know everything before they start receiving money for what they *do* know. But not you, right? You are ready to Retreat and Grow RICH! You need to start somewhere, and you want to dig deep and trust that you actually are enough and know enough to make this happen.

Just by going through the process of leading your first retreat you will grow so much that the second one will be an even greater value! In fact, if you do this work correctly, it's likely that with full integrity you can raise your prices each time you lead a retreat!

Understanding the L.E.A.R.N. approach can help you relax into your RICH Retreat and play around with new topics and content knowing it will get better and better with time!

L – **Listen to guidance.** This is the step of tuning in to and trusting your intuition about what is important to you and the message that is meant to come through you next.

E – **Engage in new conversation.** Talk to people about your new thoughts and ideas with the intention of deepening your own understanding about what you want to teach. I often do this by writing about it in my newsletter or posting on social media. I'm somewhat gauging the response of others, but even more important, checking my own passion for and alignment with the topic.

A – **Ask people to buy.** Your ideas feel great to you, but if others don't invest in the outcome you're talking about, you can't really find out how valuable it is. I recommend asking people to buy the outcome before you have it all perfectly planned out. Having paying customers creates a whole new energy for you to get it done.

R – Rally to deliver. Now fulfill on the promise of what you sold with full integrity. You might discover that the original idea or plan doesn't work quite as well as you thought. As long as you are committed to doing whatever it takes to meet the outcome, you'll learn and your clients and retreat attendees will get the value. Your intuition will kick in to find the best path, which can be a bit different from the one you originally imagined.

N – New material. After delivering your program or retreat, review what happened and turn your best stuff into new material for marketing your next retreat! I always test my ideas in retreats before I share them more broadly.

While it seems like the ideal outcome of this chapter and the next would be to know *exactly* what you'll do every minute of your retreat, remember to leave space to LEARN. No matter how much we secretly want to control everything, business development is an organic process, and you will have way more fun if you give it the space and intuitive growth process it deserves.

What's Your Retreat Actually About?

Now it's time to take a look at what your retreat is actually *about*! Finally! You've outlined your HLP; now let's look back at the big picture of the rooms in your castle.

Pull out the map of your castle. Based on your knowledge of your work, and especially based on having mapped out the specific work you did or would do with your three clients, what do your STAR clients need to know, do, achieve, or realize *first*? This is the topic of your RR. It's the piece of your container of support that takes them to an actual result and shows them that having more support in their lives will really benefit them. This is your goal for your RR.

There are two types of RRs. There is the *Castle Tour* and there is the *House Party*. As you define what your retreat is actually about, you will also choose which type resonates with you the most.

The **Castle Tour** guides participants through an overview of the steps they need to follow to get to the destination. It is, just as it sounds, a tour through the second floor of your castle. You will walk your retreat participants through each step of the process during your retreat.

Because this is a process that normally takes months with your private clients, you will not be able to go deep in each room. You'll stop in each room; cover how they would implement that step, perhaps through doing an exercise; then move to the next room. You provide the *what* but not much of the *how* for each of the steps in your process. When they leave your retreat they will know the three to five steps they need to focus on to get a result, but they will not have necessarily gotten all the way to the destination. Some will take it and run with it, and others will want your HLP for further support.

Then there is the **House Party**. I love a good party. Have you ever noticed that 90 percent of the guests at a house party congregate in the kitchen? Perhaps this is because food is often the focus of a party.

The House Party retreat is inspired by this kind of gathering. Invite people to your castle; give them a cursory tour, saying here's this room, here's that room, and here's the other room; and then show them the room that represents the first or most important step in your process and tell them, "This is what we really care about today, so this is where we're going to hang out." You briefly orient your participants to the full process of getting from the bus stop to the destination, then quickly focus them in on the first or most important step/room, having summarized the rest. You will go deep and help them get a solid result from the content of that first room or step. They will know from your summary that there are four more rooms they want to explore with you.

Castle Tour Example

Mary Beth was an attendee at my Retreat and Grow Rich Essentials LIVE retreat. She is a healer who had developed a successful business using online marketing to connect with clients. She was getting older and she wanted to use what she'd learned to establish a business that required less of her time. She wanted to hang out more with her grandkids, and while she wasn't sure she'd ever retire, she wanted that option.

Many of the healing techniques she'd used to heal herself and her clients she'd developed on her own. People went to her when their doctors couldn't help or even make a diagnosis. The work of doing these techniques one on one was super rewarding for her, but also demanding of her energy. She'd spent the last forty-plus years of her life using her techniques to heal and didn't want what she'd learned to die with her. It was time to go back out into the world and share all that she'd discovered.

Mary Beth had hosted some small retreats in her home. She had intuitively found her way to this approach, and the work was definitely guided by Spirit. She usually invited four attendees and followed Spirit as the weekend unfolded. She had no agenda or intended outcome other than healing.

She attended my retreat because she wanted to host larger retreats away from home to pass on her healing knowledge and train others in how to become healers. She'd always simply followed her intuition in her retreats and didn't know exactly how to structure her new retreat vision.

We did the exercise of content-mapping the steps Mary Beth took with her favorite clients. While she'd been primarily selling single sessions or session bundles, her favorite clients generally bought multiple times from her, and she was able to map out their healing journeys.

What was unique about Mary Beth's content mapping was that we didn't need to structure the healing work better, rather we needed to structure how she might TEACH SOMEONE ELSE how to do the work. She was able to see that there was definitely a method to her madness, and that there were very specific steps that she took with her clients. We began to see a system emerge. We could see that in her HLP, which was some form of certification, she would teach certain steps via live retreats and others via virtual training. We could also see that she would give her students space to practice the techniques between retreats and trainings. To learn Mary Beth's approach, which she had developed into a multiple-six-figure business working from home, would require her students to invest a significant amount of time and money. She wanted to offer it to select STAR clients who would learn the value via an RR. How could she bring in the right people, give them solid value, and create a natural gateway to becoming a healer?

Because the HLP would teach clients a multitude of healing techniques and foundational principles, it was important that those who attended the RR would get a taste of what they would learn in the HLP. She needed to show them the big picture of what it would take to become a healer. So the House Party – going deep in a single topic – wasn't the right approach. For example, "reintegration" was one of the rooms of Mary Beth's castle. If she focused on that single piece of the puzzle, her attendees wouldn't get a full sense of what becoming a healer in her HLP would entail.

A Castle Tour was going to be the best approach. Mary Beth had a large list of past clients and people who had heard her teach before, and many of them were drawn to her because they, too, were healers and interested in healing. Because the intention of the retreat was to launch her healer certification program, we wanted to be as transparent as possible and attract the most targeted group possible. We developed her retreat as a Castle Tour that we tentatively named "Am I a Healer?" It overviewed the three foundational techniques for her approach to healing on day one, covered the life and business of being a healer on day two so they could start to picture themselves doing that work, and then day three included integrating what they'd learned, some self-healing work, and making the decision about whether they wanted to take the next step as healers.

Based on Mary Beth's understanding of her audience (and mine, as I also consider myself a healer through business), we really knew that there were plenty of people out there asking, "Am I a Healer?" Remember that great marketing completes the thought that is already emerging in your prospect's mind. The Castle Tour made perfect sense for her intention to lead her clients into her HLP. Let them see the whole big picture, then give them the opportunity to invest in the support they needed to learn, practice, implement, become certified, and turn it into a business!

House Party Example

The Inner Alignment Intensive I hosted for years was a House Party. My HLP at the time was called the Profit Acceleration Circle, and I wanted to use the Inner Alignment Intensive to bring clients into that program. I wanted a retreat that pushed boundaries and was truly transformational for my attendees. My prior retreat, The Sweet Spot Business Intensive, included experiences and games to facilitate learning, but it also covered a lot of ground (remember my 182 PowerPoint slides?). The Sweet Spot Business Intensive was a Castle Tour in which I taught participants at a high level everything from how to identify their sweet spot in business to how to package, price, and market it. It was *a lot*.

At the end of the weekend the attendees who resonated with my approach knew they were going to need help implementing all they had learned, so The Sweet Spot Business Intensive was a natural bridge to the Profit Acceleration Circle. However, I wanted to go deeper in my teaching. I also got a little bored with teaching all that marketing stuff, and wanted to make a change. I went back to the drawing board. I did exactly what I have my clients do today, putting all my steps out on Post-its. I looked at my castle and I asked myself, "What do my clients need to know, do, or embody *first* such that they will be ready to do all the rest?" And the subsequent question was "What do I need my clients to buy into to make them perfect clients for me?"

Everything I was teaching at the time boiled down to the five categories (rooms of my castle) that I shared in the last chapter. I knew I didn't want people's introduction to me to be in the area of marketing; I wanted my retreat to center around a core piece of the work that would be most effective when delivered as a live experience. And I wanted to go deep.

My unique gift is in being able to see and understand someone's value and match it to the market that wants it. But more important, I actually help them understand their value and start treating themselves as if they are valuable, thus teaching others to value them. I am a healer of old, painful belief systems that lead to taking your value for granted.

Based on what I knew was my very best work, and knowing this was the work I believed was most fundamental and important to all the other work, I decided on a House Party in the room of "Owning Your Value."

I called my retreat Inner Alignment Intensive: Raise Your Rates While Staying True to You. The intention of the retreat was for each person to own their value deep down in their bones. I did this through a structured series of conversations about value and substance and an exercise that caused participants to EXPERIENCE their relationships to value and money and their resistance to receiving. If someone didn't shift their belief system about their value through this work, they probably were not going to be ready to be an HLP client, as my HLP clients are all premium providers and committed to owning their greatness, even when it's hard to do so.

Those who attended the Inner Alignment Intensive were ready to take themselves and their businesses on at deeper levels, and all the other steps became more valuable. Even those who already had coaches or other containers of support got great value from the retreat. This is what you're looking for when you design a House Party type of RR.

So will your retreat be a House Party or a Castle Tour? Here's a side-by-side list so you can see which features are the best fit for you:

A HOUSE PARTY is for you if…	A CASTLE TOUR is for you if…
• You love to go deep with everyone and get to the heart of a pattern that they can transform.	• You prefer people have a clear understanding of the big picture of your work.
• It's very hard for you to stay surfacy and to not tell people everything you know about a topic.	• You are very good at teaching a linear process.
• There is a room in your castle that you clearly love the most – that truly represents your unique gifts.	• You can stick to the high-level "what" in sharing information about a room without succumbing to the urge to share all the "hows" and risk overwhelming people.
• You can see that until your clients address the first room, the rest of the work will fall on deaf ears.	• You love teaching all the rooms in your castle equally and you wouldn't enjoy the retreat yourself if you left some out.
• You feel excited about marketing the transformation of one room in particular.	• The STAR client for your HLP needs to buy in to the full process in order to say yes to your HLP, and you need the full two-and-a-half days to share the full process.
• You are a nonlinear thinker and prefer to have the freedom and flexibility to play within one room, putting the pieces together to get to an outcome.	• You like the idea of, or your type of work requires, people making a conscious commitment to your program knowing exactly what they will get and what is expected of them.
• You like the idea of, or your type of work requires, people making a leap of faith in working with you without necessarily knowing all the steps. (This requires great integrity on your part and can often result in larger transformation because transformation always stems from faith.)	

You should now have a feel for which type of retreat is best for you. You can always try out different approaches as you determine what works best for you and your clients! I've done both House Parties and Castle Tours with equal success. Yet I always tend toward the go-deep approach of the House Party when I don't have a specific reason to go broad with the Castle Tour. What about you?

EXERCISE:

Your Retreat Type

Review the rooms of your castle and make a decision as to whether your RR will be a House Party or a Castle Tour. This will help you to take the first step toward structuring the flow of content and experiences.

If you've chosen a Castle Tour, begin to speculate about the order in which you'd like to tour your rooms. Cover one to two rooms on day one, two rooms on day two, and one room on day three. Place the most powerful, most transformational, or most eye-opening room on the first day in the afternoon.

> I include actual retreat agenda templates in my virtual training course. You can grab them as a bonus at **RetreatandGrowRich.com/agendas**.

If you've chosen a House Party, which room of your castle will be the focus of your RR? Go ahead and choose – trust yourself and move forward!

You've decided on your retreat type – congrats! In the next chapter we're going to look at the STRUCTURE of your RR. Some of you will be pleasantly surprised to learn that you can actually structure a retreat with *no* content!

Chapter 9

Your RICH Retreat, Part II — The Three Retreat Structures

I was standing in front of the room, crying. It had been quite some time since my last good public cry. I'd been in business for a few years and things were flowing. My business was generating multiple six figures, and I could essentially work from home in my pajamas. Every freedom-seeker's dream, right?

Yet there I was, unable to hold myself together. It was the second day of a retreat I was attending as a client, and it was my turn in front of the room in the "hot seat." I was to share with the group about where I was and where I wanted to be so that I could get input from my coach and the room about how to get where I wanted to go. So simple. Yet there I stood so frustrated I was unable to speak, which led to the tears.

I had no idea what I wanted in that moment. I'd created everything I'd thought of creating in terms of my personal income and freedom, and I didn't know what was next.

It was then that my coach suggested a tool I'd not heard of before called Human Design, and gave me a referral to an expert who could guide me. I was grateful for her intuition and followed her guidance. (It was rare that she had such specific woo-woo guidance so I knew to pay attention.)

The Human Design System is based on astrology and the i-Ching. I had my Human Design "read" and participated in a two-part call to explain the report to me. The first thing I learned was that I am not actually designed to know what I want. The reason I had been so frustrated by the assignment of sharing what I wanted next was that it hadn't actually revealed itself yet! My Human Design report revealed that I never know what I want until I see it and resonate with it. There are often lulls in my vision when I haven't yet been exposed to the thing I want next. This is part of why I'm continually exposing myself to new ideas and experiences so that I can allow my leadership to grow.

I learned many other details about how I am designed as well, but the one that stands out is one of the reasons I love retreats and want to help lay the foundation for choosing your retreat structure. What follows is a *very* brief glimpse into Human Design, but it could be helpful.

Our Human Design is made up of nine energy centers. Each center is either open or closed. Open centers indicate that you easily pick up on other people's energy – thoughts, desires, feelings, voice, etc. – as it relates to that specific center. Closed centers indicate you have your own fixed ways in those areas. I have an open center in my design that allows me to give voice to what others need to hear to move forward. I am designed to wake people up to their purpose using this skill. Because of this I am much better off – more aligned and on purpose – when I develop a retreat with *less* content and more space to give voice to what needs to be heard. This is why the retreat approach works so well for me and why I often veer toward one specific retreat structure, as I'll share with you shortly.

While I am not yet an expert in the Human Design System, I now have my clients get their Human Design reports done (I recommend HumanDesignForUsAll.com). It is highly likely that you have open centers like mine. They make you able to intuitively pick up on who people are, what they need, what they desire, what they are thinking, or what they are feeling. This is why you'll be so magical in a retreat setting! You will help reveal to your participants the missing links that they can't see on their own!

Creating transformation in groups is a spot-on strategy! We often can't see what we need to know to grow without the complementary channels of others! Consider how big a role this intuitive knowing will play in your own retreat. Will you leave space in your agenda for guiding individuals or the group as a whole in giving voice to or expressing the emotion of that which has been previously unsaid or unfelt; or are you better designed for a pre-planned, fixed experience?

Most people are aware at some level of their intuitive gifts, but your Human Design report can verify them for you and make you more confident in molding your retreat around your intuitions. Trust yourself as you choose your retreat structure in this chapter.

Circling back to the resolution of my tears in front of the room... shortly after being in that hot seat and learning about my Human Design, my next desire showed up. I began seeing images of mountains everywhere I turned. I paid attention to this desire to explore mountains, and shortly thereafter booked a month-long rental in Colorado. The following year I relocated. There I met the love of my life, and the next level of my journey unfolded. Because of a random intuitive hit that surfaced for my coach while I was at that retreat, my life has never been the same. In the environment of like-minded entrepreneurs with intentions for transformation, I was given the next piece in my puzzle of alignment. It wasn't complicated. It didn't come from a magic formula or an in-depth content structure. It was a moment of vulnerability on my part and intuition on my coach's part, that led to a ripple effect of decisions, that led me to share this with you today.

This will happen for your clients and retreat participants as well, so let's structure for it, shall we?

The Three Retreat Structures

You've decided whether you are a Castle-Tour or a House-Party type of person. This has allowed you to determine the focus of your RR so you know how to market it and can think through the content you'd like to share. You have one more decision to make about structure, and this is a fun one as well!

There are three ways to structure the activities and agenda of your retreat:

1) Content Retreat
2) Mastermind Retreat
3) Combo Retreat

Just like it sounds, a *content retreat* is structured around your content. It moves from one piece of content to the next, or one exercise or experience to the next. To be clear, this doesn't mean that you can't improvise, ad-lib, and change things up. That is always your right and responsibility as a transformational retreat leader. However, based on the promised outcome of the retreat and what you want to accomplish, you need to keep the flow structured and on track. My Retreat and Grow Rich Essentials LIVE retreat is a content retreat. Because I work with the group to develop their own RRs over the course of three days, I need to have everyone moving in the same direction at the same time. It is a full-on content retreat.

A *mastermind retreat* is the exact opposite. Rather than being structured around content, there is likely only *one* piece of content, which is your introduction to the topic (either a high-level tour of your castle or an introduction to the "kitchen" of your house party). A mastermind retreat is generated entirely by the participants. Based on the way you position and market your retreat, your participants come together with a specific intention or outcome in mind, or all having a similar problem. Your marketing positions your retreat to help them solve that specific problem and get to the intended outcome, and each participant brings with them the problem they most want to solve. You set up your participants with the intention of creating that outcome, and the combined minds of the group form a *master* mind that guides the process of getting that result – through you. You are the guide who asks the questions, and everybody in the room learns from how you help each person solve their problem. Leaving time for your introduction each day, you divide the number of hours in the retreat by the number of people in the room, and each person has a segment of time in front of the room. This time is often referred to as the hot seat, though I prefer to call it a laser-coaching session.

If you've ever experienced someone else receiving expert coaching in front of a room, you know how beneficial this is to witness, because each participant asks things you might never think to ask. When not in the hot seat yourself, you are more likely to let your defenses down and receive insight. That's the premise of the mastermind retreat.

This type of retreat is also often called a *business intensive* and various other names. If you go this route, you'll want to decide whether your retreat is a true mastermind, in which you are simply an equal participant with everyone else in the room and all people contribute, or you will be the coach and the floor is opened up only at your permission. For the purposes of growing your business and ensuring the intended outcome, I recommend you be the coach, especially if there is a wide range of people in your room.

A *combo retreat* simply combines the two. It's roughly 50 percent content and 50 percent mastermind, combining the best of both worlds. You guide certain portions of the content and let the participants generate the rest. It's often an ideal balance of controlling and allowing. You structure your retreat such that specific teachings and experiences happen at specific times, provide the room with valuable content, and set aside time for each attendee to have their burning question answered by you in front of the room. You decide how the rest of the attendees participate in these sessions. Estimate how much time your content and transformational experience will take, and do the math to determine how much of the remaining time each person's laser-coaching session (hot seat) will take. If you have six hours of time available and twelve participants, each person gets roughly half an hour. (Schedule twenty minutes to have time for wrap-up and transition between people.)

I structured my Inner Alignment Intensive as a combo retreat. It's a great way to leverage your time by teaching core concepts to the whole room, creating experiences for individuals to step into transformation and ensuring they get their burning questions answered, while demonstrating your ability as coach and guide in an array of scenarios. In my Inner Alignment Intensive some participants asked about their business models or marketing calendars, and others asked about healing from things their parents told them as children that made them doubt their own value. The combination worked really well for addressing both the practical and the spiritual issues involved in running and creating a business.

Remember I told you early in the book that you will need less content than you think? At least half of you will choose a mastermind or combo retreat, and now you know why you need very little content!

Each type of retreat can work beautifully to meet your goals. And you can easily see the benefits and downsides of each of them listed below.

> I share actual agenda templates for each structure at
> **RetreatandGrowRich.com/agendas.**

Content Retreat	Mastermind Retreat	Combo Retreat
Benefits:	*Benefits:*	*Benefits:*
• Provides the most control of the experience. • It can be easier to feel confident that you will meet the promised outcomes because you've mapped out the entire experience. • Your marketing can paint a picture of specifically what will happen on day one, day two, etc., because you actually know! • You are definitely positioned as expert.	• Allows the most organic unfolding of what each participant needs. • There is little or no content-planning needed in advance aside from crafting your heart-connection story and one segment to set up the laser-coaching sessions. • There's ample time and space to create community. • It's easy to allow for intuitive guidance.	• Nice blend of control and faith. • There are opportunities to create community connection as participants survive the hot seat together and learn about each other. • Positions you as a content expert and also a powerful coach. • Less planning is required than for a content retreat. • It's a great model for a beginner because you can test out content and also use the laser-coaching sessions as research to see what participants need next.

Content Retreat	Mastermind Retreat	Combo Retreat
Downsides: • Requires more time to prepare content because the planning needs to be tight. • You might incur additional costs for setting up a projector or printing structured handouts. • There's less room for Spirit to guide the journey. • There can *sometimes* be less space for going deep with people, depending on the nature of the content.	*Downsides:* • Has the least amount of control. If you are not skilled at coaching in front of a room, you can easily get off track. • You are positioned as guide more than expert. Some people might take that for granted. • You might struggle with marketing if you haven't developed your faith in the power of intention.	*Downsides:* • Time for content is limited. • It requires more planning than the mastermind structure. • It requires better time management, as you need to move the bigger conversation about your content along while also managing the individual needs that surface.

Your next step will of course be to decide how you'd like to structure your RICH Retreat! Will you do a content, mastermind, or combo retreat?

LIVE IT! A Quick Guide for Structuring Your Content!

Once you've decided your retreat type and your structure, outline your detailed agenda. I recommend a two-and-a-half-day retreat, which allows your clients to experience three fresh days of energy but does not overwhelm them with three full days, allowing them to fly home on day three if desired. I break the days into ninety-minute segments with two fifteen- to thirty-minute breaks and a ninety-minute lunch break. I often include at least one evening session as well, usually on day two.

If you've chosen the mastermind structure, develop a ninety-minute segment of content to open your retreat. Leave the bulk of your final half-day open to address any themes or questions that came up. The rest of your time will be filled with laser-coaching sessions (hot seats).

For a content or combo retreat, develop segments of content that you will teach. One topic can span ninety minutes or even two ninety-minute segments.

Planning your segments can be simple! Remember to leave space for what shows up. Below is a quick guide for planning your content segments. The acronym L.I.V.E. I.T. reminds you to always be living in alignment with what you teach!

L – Lesson. The first step is to share an overview of the lesson you are sharing. This is most effectively done using a story. The story can be yours, a client's, or even something you read in the news. The story helps engage your attendees' emotions and allows them to bypass their thinking brains so they can engage at a deeper level.

I – Intention. Next share your intention for this segment of content and have attendees develop their own intentions for it. You can simply provide them with a few prompts such as, "What would be available for you if you could learn this lesson or make this change?" Have them reflect on it or write it down.

V – Verify. Check in with your attendees and verify that they have gotten what you wanted them to from the set-up of the segment. I often refer to this as "taking people with you." It can be as simple as having a few people in the room share what they wrote for their own intention, or asking, "What do you hear in this?" or "What's coming up for you?" This quick check-in establishes unity and gets everyone on the same page.

E – Experience. This is the bulk of the content for this segment. You can teach a bit here to flesh out the idea and then give them an exercise or experience to help them apply what you just taught. This can include a worksheet, a handout, or a guided journaling exercise. It can also include a partner exercise, a game, or even a physical-challenge type of experience to help them "drive up their shit" or integrate the lesson.

I – Integrate. Now give your participants a chance to integrate what they just learned through journaling in their notebooks or sharing around the room. I've done everything from having them declare their "new truths" in front of the room to having them move their bodies to help integrate the experience.

T – Take-Away/Transformation. Give attendees the opportunity to share their take-aways. Each person in the room will learn from what the others share. Depending on the depth of the segment and where it falls in your retreat, the take-away might be a transformation or it might be experiencing a profound shift to being different in the world. Not every segment ends with a transformation – this would be too much to take on in one retreat. In fact, you want to craft the flow of your content such that there is one main segment that is transformational in nature.

I love helping people craft the flow of their content so that the transformational experience is in the exact perfect place to create the best outcome. This is both an art and a science that I partner with my clients to master. It's likely you have a pretty strong intuition about how to do this. If you run into trouble, please email my team!

Naming, Pricing, and Filling Your Retreat

Now it's time to name and price your RR. The topic of filling your retreat with attendees could easily fill its own book, as there is an abundance of ways to market both in person and online.

The details of Internet launches, sponsorships, and speaking engagements are outside the scope of this book, but I share a few important tips below.

Naming

same as coaching program?

The most important factor when it comes to naming your RR is that you love the name. Remember that when it comes to your retreat, you want what you are doing, what you are saying, and who you are being to all be in alignment. You want to feel totally excited when you talk about your retreat and to know that what you'll be doing is in full alignment with how you talk about it.

Your name will not make or break your retreat! In the beginning you'll be registering people through one-on-one conversations, and after a few retreats you'll be masterful at doing this. I filled my Inner Alignment Intensive for three-and-a-half years. No one actually wanted their inners aligned, and I didn't follow any guidelines in coming up with that name, but it still worked out just fine.

Your name should include both DESTINATION and INSPIRATION. It should include a specific, tangible benefit or outcome that participants get at the destination, and have an aspirational bent to it. You get to create a name for your retreat, and then a tagline, so you should have enough space to satisfy these requirements. Luckily I had room to play with a tagline for the Inner Alignment Intensive, and I settled on "Raise Your Rates While Staying True to You," which you can see has a descriptive outcome.

Think of yourself standing at the destination saying to everyone, "Hey guys, it's awesome over here. Come join me!" That's the kind of declaration you want to make with your name such that it draws people in.

Pricing

You have a lot of flexibility when it comes to pricing. Because you will be generating clients from this retreat and it's the first step in the bigger picture of their work with you, you don't have to overthink the pricing. Here are the things to consider when pricing your retreat:

- The price should be high enough that your STAR client feels invested. Because most of my clients host retreats that people need to travel to, their attendees are already buying plane tickets; so that is an investment already, and you can keep your retreat price relatively low. However, if you have a client who is used to spending money and would not take your offer seriously unless it was priced in the multi-thousands or even five figures, price it higher for that client than you normally would for most people.

- Ensure that your registration fees will cover the cost to host your retreat even if it doesn't fill up. I recommend setting your pricing so that the retreat breaks even if it is half full. A typical RR that I host costs me roughly $4,000, and twelve participants is what I generally consider to be full. So if I want to break even at six people, I need to charge at least $667. Your retreat will cost more or less depending on the choices you make.

> I'm not covering logistics in this book, though there is an extensive logistics module in my training program at **RetreatandGrowRich.com/Course.**

I charged $297 for my first retreat – the one that made me $36,000 on the back end through the upsell to my HLP. I later charged $1,497, and discovered that anyone who would pay $1,497 would also pay $1,997, and eventually increased the investment.

Don't overthink it! If you are not going to offer an HLP for clients to continue with you after your retreat, charge a higher price for your retreat. A low price reduces the barrier to entry and helps you reach your ultimate goal of having a full HLP.

Filling

I teach how to market your business in my HLP, but here are a few tips:

- For your first retreat you will likely need to talk with your prospects one on one to have them say yes. This is great news for two reasons. The first is that you will learn a great deal by talking to them. It will help you be even better at delivering the outcome in your retreat. Think of it as research. The second is that when you talk to people you don't have to waste time writing a retreat website! It's great to have a website, but you can spend weeks writing and spending a lot of money creating it, and that keeps you from hosting or at least filling your retreat right now! Embrace this opportunity to hone your one-on-one selling skills through these phone calls or meetings.

- Start marketing your retreat at least eight weeks in advance. If you plan to create a comprehensive online marketing campaign, give yourself another four to eight weeks to plan and execute it. And of course, the earlier you start enrolling, the better. Provide an incentive for registering at least three weeks in advance so you can more easily plan your room set-up and food and beverage orders. The incentive can be a price increase after the early registration, or bonus coaching with you that expires after early registration. I've found that a group of registrations comes in six to eight weeks prior and a second group comes in close to the date of the retreat. If you don't give them a motivation to decide, they will wait until the week or even the day before! If you can give yourself more than eight weeks, that's even better.

- Test out your retreat-naming ideas by hosting teleclasses or webinars. If you're not sure which one of your brainstormed names is the most effective, you can host a different class each week or month using the different names to gauge the responses. You can get some practice teaching in these classes as well. While it's not an exact representation, it will give you a pretty good idea of how your audience will respond to the energy of the words you choose. You can market these classes to your list if you have a subscriber base, or via Facebook ads, or even by asking your friends and connections to share it on social media. Leadpages is the tool I use to quickly tell me how many people visit my pages and what percentage choose to register. You can offer free strategy sessions with you as a bonus for signing up for a class, and convert those people into paying retreat attendees... even if you haven't yet chosen the name of your retreat!

- Start with marketing to all current and past clients if you have them. Offer reduced or even complimentary registrations to clients and past clients. These are the people who will help you get critical mass and momentum for your program. If you don't yet have any clients, consider bringing in your initial clients before your first retreat so you can get some cash flow and experience, offer the retreat as a bonus when they sign on as a client, and confirm their attendance. I recommend offering initial clients a short-term program such as a three-month bundle of sessions or a VIP Day with you, and include admission to the retreat. This would be your beginning Gateway Program.

- If your current and past clients say no to your retreat, rethink your retreat topic (unless you've completely pivoted course in your business). If those who already know and trust you don't register for free or at a discount, there could be a marketing issue — for example, the destination hasn't been made sufficiently clear.

- You will eventually fill your retreats exclusively from people who have taken your Gateway! They have already engaged with you; know, like, and trust you; and will register without hesitancy when they realize how awesome it will be to be in the room with you! I'll show you why and how in the next chapter.

EXERCISE:

Your Retreat Structure

If you haven't done so yet, choose the structure of your RR. Will you use the content, mastermind, or combo structure to direct the flow of your experience? Begin to map out your content in ninety-minute segments using the template below. If so inspired, give your retreat a name and select the date for your first retreat!

	Day 1	Day 2	Day 3
A.M.			
Segment 1			
Break			
Segment 2			
LUNCH			
Segment 3			
Break			
Segment 4			
DINNER			
Optional Evening Session			

Want to simplify your agenda planning process?

Download our RICH Retreat agenda templates at
retreatandgrowrich.com/agendas

Way to go! You've made the key decisions about your RICH Retreat and have begun to lay out your agenda. In the next chapter I share my top tips for BEING THE LEADER of your retreat room and expertly guiding your participants to the desired outcome. See you there!

Chapter 10

Your Room Wants a Leader

It was fall of 2002. The school year had just started. It was my second year as a high school teacher at Clark Montessori High School, the first public Montessori high school in the country. I was dressed in my conservative "teacher clothes," probably khaki pants and a button-up shirt – ugh! – that I thought I needed to wear to fit the part.

If you're not familiar with the Montessori educational approach, it's centered around experiential learning, or more specifically, having students "discover" their own lessons in a context that supports a specific outcome.

Teaching was a tough gig for me – the structured hours and minute-to-minute routines, the many students we served that were in very challenging circumstances at home, and attempting to teach math, which had always come easily to me, to students for whom it didn't. However, if I were going to teach anywhere, Clark was by far the best school for me and my growth.

At Clark we took two weeks off from regular classes twice a year to do immersion learning in courses called Intersessions. Students paid for these courses, and our goal was to offer a variety of options at different price points, as we had students from all socioeconomic backgrounds at Clark. The most extravagant option was the annual trip to Andros Island in the Bahamas. The most basic (and inexpensive) was the Job Internship and Community Service option, which was essentially free. Each fall, teachers signed up for the two Intersessions they would lead or co-lead during the year. As a new teacher I was assigned to Job Internship and Community Service in year one. The students shadowed someone in a career of interest during the first week, and we checked on them. In the second week we planted garlic and weeded gardens at a non-profit farm in the community.

I led four Intersessions in my two years as a full-time teacher. The second year I led a civil rights tour, which was a two-week road trip to historical sites in the South (Selma, Montgomery, Birmingham, Tuskegee, etc.), and an eleven-day backpacking trip on the Appalachian Trail in Georgia. As you can imagine, these trips were ripe with learning experiences and opportunities to grow. From emotional discussions about race relations in a mixed-race group of students to journaling about the experience of hiking, eating, and bathing in the backwoods, these experiences were life-changing. (And isn't it amazing that I magically landed in a role that allowed me to do these things and plant seeds for my future career?) Yet I want to tell you about my favorite Intersession that changed who I was forever and led me to understand how to lead a room.

I'd decided to apply to run my own Intersession that fall of my second year at Clark. I didn't know what it would be about, but the criteria that would make it worth doing for me personally were:

1) A low enrollment fee so that any student would be able to register

2) Interesting enough that even students who had money would want to register

3) An environment that would promote open and truthful discussions

4) Specifically designed to connect students of different socioeconomic and cultural backgrounds such that they would discover that they have more in common than not; that is, they would discover a love of diversity

Based on the above criteria, I'd brainstormed a list of four different options for topics and began surveying students in the lunchroom, hallways, and study halls, putting my former marketing research skills to work. I have to tell you, I was nervous about what I was up to. Sure they were students, and I was the teacher and therefore in charge, but what if they didn't like any of the ideas? What if I was getting in over my head? What if my vision didn't work?

To disclose a bit more about my nervousness, I need to take you back to my first year in teaching. I'd left my role as senior engineer to teach high school. A few months into it I had the same complaints about the new job that I'd had about the old one. That's when I decided I needed to do something to change *me*. I took a transformational training program in which I learned a lot about myself and my judgments that were creating the "Groundhog Day" experience.

I also learned how to create an intention for an outcome I wanted and then live as if the outcome was certain to happen. It was a concept I'd been practicing over the year, and it had changed my experience of my day-to-day life. I'd invented more optimistic ways of interpreting other people's behaviors and saw these behaviors in a new light. I'd set intentions for how I wanted to show up in certain meetings and friendships, and I'd watched things unfold exactly as I intended or better. I'd been secretly building my intention "muscle."

Now it was time to put this new way of thinking to the test. Could I spend two weeks with a group of students and have them walk away with a changed perspective of how they viewed themselves and one another? Could I actually lead a group to a transformation?

"Cooking Across Cultures" is the Intersession name that won the vote by a landslide, and the real planning began. I planned to use Internet videos to teach basic knife skills and have the kids practice in the classroom. Then one of my fellow teachers, Cate, volunteered her home kitchen. She had a beautiful oversized professional kitchen within walking distance of the school! I enlisted friends from my Procter & Gamble days who were from other countries and loved cooking. There was even a professional who taught Chinese cooking classes at Procter & Gamble's culinary center. Each guest chef taught us one or two recipes from their culture – from potstickers to samosas – and as we enjoyed our food they shared stories about what it was like around the dinner table in their cultures and what their household customs were growing up. My Indian guest chef brought a photo album from her wedding and told us about the extensive multi-day event.

One of my math students was a true Italian, and her parents invited us to their home to cook pasta from scratch. We dined at local ethnic restaurants and took the bus to Findley Market, the local farmers market, where the kids were to locate certain ingredients and explore the various ethnic groceries.

During the second week each person partnered up with someone from a different food culture with the assignment to go each other's homes for dinner. They were to report back on their experiences. And the two weeks culminated in a food expo we called A Taste of Clark in which each of them cooked a dish that was popular in their family and created a display about their food culture.

It was a fun-filled two weeks, and the experiences were profound. I tear up every time I think about it. It moves me because today I still believe in the underlying intention of letting your guard down and connecting. Food was an amazing vehicle for this! Students formed unlikely friendships from the experience. One student found his calling, and now owns his own restaurant in San Francisco. But what moves me the most is that one person can lead a group to a profound transformation through the simple power of holding clear intention.

I didn't market my Intersession as "The Diversity Course." I didn't tell anyone that the goal was to go out into life as adults slightly less prejudiced. I didn't have the kids study the history of racism or overtly confront the beliefs and judgments they'd inherited from their families. Yet through the energy with which I structured what I designed, showed up, led the retreat, and asked questions, the students got the outcome I desired. It was powerful learning that I carry with me to this day.

What is the outcome you desire for your clients, whether overtly stated or not? What is the mission you're on? And who do you need to *be* in front of the room for that outcome to become real for your participants?

The Power of Intention

The first thing to understand about leading your room is the power of intention. Dr. Wayne Dyer wrote a phenomenal book, that I read often, called *The Power of Intention*. The description of the book on its publisher's website says:

> The power of intention is the energy that surrounds us all, and allows us to accomplish our life's goal. Self-help master Dr. Wayne Dyer tells us how we can train ourselves to tune into this source energy and step beyond our minds and egos. When we do this, we become what Dyer calls "Connectors" and make ourselves available to the energy of success. Connectors are the people whom everyone sees as lucky, those for whom success seems effortless. They trust an invisible force that will be all-providing and they just don't attract negativity to themselves. You'll realize that fulfilling your desires is a matter of embracing this force rather than struggling uphill. This book is full of dynamic steps that we can all use to tap into the transformational energy of the all-creating Source.

This is exactly what happened as I led my Cooking Across Cultures course to the outcome I desired, and it will be a key principle for you as you develop your RR.

Merriam-Webster defines *intention* as "a determination to act in a certain way; what one intends to bring about." Be intentional about your leadership of your retreat. There are three ways to approach setting an intention. You can set an intention that is a specific, measureable outcome, such as "I'd like to make $10,000" or "I'd like to attract three ideal clients." You can set an intention for an outcome that is more qualitative in nature, such as "I'd like to establish my brand as a leader in the world of transformational retreats" or "I'd like people to gain insight about how they have been keeping themselves from achieving their goals." And most powerful, an intention can be set as a way of being or a word or phrase that represents how you want to show up energetically. While awareness of who we are being is becoming a popular topic, many people don't know what that means, so I'll elaborate.

Pause right now, as you are reading, and ask yourself, "Who am I being right now?" What are the first things that pop into your mind? If I were to play along, I might respond with a title: "I'm being a *writer*." Examples of other titles I might think of are *leader, CEO, mother, community-builder, lover, partner, friend*. I might also say I am being "*committed*" – I'm showing up to write when I could be going for a hike or watching episodes of *Chopped* on TV. I'm also being *intentional* about helping you understand the real power behind your profitable retreat; *inspired* because I'm thinking of this book in your hands and imagining what you might do next; and possibly a bit *distracted* because it's Saturday afternoon and I've been writing for five hours; I now have three beverages and three electronic screens open at my desk along with a crystal and a handful of angel cards and I'm itching to get moving! But thus far *inspired* and *committed* are winning out!

We have the power to choose who we are being in each moment. We mostly don't use this power and instead just remain who we've always been. Who we are being creates our world. Dr. Dyer also said, "You don't attract what you want. You attract what you are."

When you lead your retreat, be deliberate about who you are being as much or even more than what you are teaching. Your *beingness* creates the energy in the room. Your attendees will entrain to, or get in harmony with, your energy, and thus your intentionality helps ease their personal transformations. I teach more about this in my online courses, and especially in my live retreats, so my students can more deeply understand the principles involved. (I'm already feeling that might be my next book!)

The main thing to understand is that you create the energy in the room through the power of your intention and who you are being. Create who you will be at your RR as a BREAKTHROUGH ENERGY that excites you, inspires you, and even makes you just a little nervous so you can show up in all of your power. You are not the teacher on high who is coming down to inform your attendees of all of this brilliance; you are actually *being* the outcome in action. You are modeling what is possible and playing for your own best life right along with them! When you are expanding and growing as the leader, they will expand and grow as participants.

The Three Intentions

I recommend you set three intentions for your retreat. The combination ensures your very best possible outcome:

1. **Intention for you.** This is the way you will be, as described above – playful, inspired, bold, challenging, serious, encouraging, loving, vulnerable, real, risk-taker, leader, etc.

2. **Intention for your participants**. There are lots of things you want your participants to learn, but what is the most important thing you intend them to leave with? In my Cooking Across Cultures course it was that people from different backgrounds are a lot like them. In my most recent retreat my intention was that participants see their value and recognize that they already were the person to deliver it; they experienced trusting themselves and their own intuition as a leader. Even

though I often use the same content in my retreats, I always set a fresh intention as I tune in to the energy and needs of the participants.

3. **Intention for your business.** This is probably the number of clients you want to convert, the amount of money you want to receive, or positioning your brand if you are in a time of transition — as in "to be seen as an expert in _____."

Captivating Your Room

A skill to develop as a retreat leader and a marketer, and really for life in general, is to captivate. Merriam-Webster defines *captivate* as "to attract and hold the attention of." It makes sense that you'd want to captivate your room, and those on your subscriber list (and your lover!).

Here's what's cool: being intentional makes you captivating. When you live up to your three intentions you have an energy of clarity that draws people in.

Many people go through life these days constantly overwhelmed, moving from one thing they "should" do to another, often with very little intention. When you're aligned with your intentions, you are rare and therefore valuable. You stand out.

Being captivating is not about being a particular way. There are as many paths to alignment as there are people. Being captivating is being fully present with an energy of intention, period.

You can visit **RetreatandGrowRich.com/captivate** to find my ten-part article series on the top ten ways to up your Captivation Factor!

Move an Individual, Move the Room

How do you lead your room to a breakthrough? It's a challenge when your participants have different goals and concerns. I've learned to focus on individual breakthroughs. This art is learned over time, which is why we practice different scenarios in my retreats so clients can experience feeling the energy shifts in the room.

I've written a bit about energy dynamics and the idea that the exact right group of people gathers in your room for each retreat. Whether or not they say it or even know it, your participants have common transformations in store for them. However, if you focus on *everyone* getting it you will not be able to go deep enough for *anyone* to get it. (More on this in chapter 13.)

Even if you're already great at teaching and leading exercises, there is no substitute for watching an individual transform before your eyes. Within the flow of your agenda there will be perfect times to invite a participant to share more deeply about what is going on for them. As you coach that individual to a breakthrough and into a new realm of what's possible, every person in the room hears a part of themselves in the other's story, reflects on their own life and work, and is moved into a new energy right along with them.

This is what makes a transformational retreat so magical. Often we can't see what we need to address and shift in our lives. We see our lives through the exact same filters every day. When we're trying to solve a particular problem, we can't see the one limiting belief that causes us to try the wrong solutions over and over again. But when someone else shares how they view a similar problem and its solution, we can suddenly see what we haven't seen before. And it's much easier to let new thoughts in when it's not about us! All our defenses go down when we experience someone else being vulnerable in front of the whole room, and we can take in the transformation.

When you are able to expertly guide someone to a new solution, others in the room change as well without your working with them or even knowing they have changed. Move an individual, move the room.

Create an Experience

No one has ever profoundly changed their life by thinking about it. Yes, our thoughts create our feelings, which create our actions (and the energy behind them), which dictate our outcomes; yet just creating a new thought does not create permanent, lasting transformation. Only experience has the power to transform.

Transformation has to do with the conscious and subconscious mind and the roles they play in how we operate. Many have written about this topic, so I'll cover it only lightly as I'm guessing you've read about or studied it yourself.

Your subconscious mind rules you most of the time. When you're not consciously choosing how you want to be, your subconscious takes over. However conscious you intend to be, this happens. A lot.

Your subconscious mind is programmed by your experiences until roughly the age of seven, when you develop the ability to choose what you want to accept or reject. All the beliefs about life you're exposed to before that age become your default beliefs – before you are old enough to understand them or choose them for yourself!

You then spend your life piling up experiences that are consistent with your subconscious worldview. You gather all kinds of evidence for why you're right about yourself, others, and the world at large. Continuing to see the world in the same way helps you feel safe and in control. Many of those views were developed in response to a perceived lack of safety, so continuing to believe them feels like the best way to stay safe.

Eventually you get frustrated that your life never changes, and as I mentioned earlier, you might experience "Groundhog Day," as in the movie, reliving variations on the same theme, and the outcome doesn't change substantially. You might think you want something different, but your subconscious mind has been running the show to keep you safe for so long that you cannot actually imagine allowing yourself to be different. You believe that as long as you stay the same and keep living life in the same way, you can pretty much predict your results. Even if you don't like the results, being able to predict them feels much better than having no idea how life might go.

This is what is happening for your retreat participants, whether they know it or not, whether they say they have it all together or not. There is some pattern that has been running the show for them for so long that they don't know who they would be without it. Changing that pattern is the real reason they have come to you. They know that if they can change the pattern, they will be able to create in a whole new way. Are you with me?

But they can't change a pattern just by thinking about it. I teach an in-depth ten-step process that I call "The Anatomy of a Transformation." Here is the short version of what is required to happen beyond just thinking about it in order for your clients to change:

1) They must become aware of the old pattern/view/belief/way of being that has been keeping them stuck.
2) They must accept that what the pattern/view/belief/way of being costs them is greater than their fear of change.
3) They must give themselves a new experience.

When someone doesn't get to step three, they inevitably revert back to their old pattern, because only experiencing themselves in a new way (and living it!) has the power to convince their subconscious that the change they seek is available and safe. The experience is the transformation.

This is why experiential live retreats are so important and, when done correctly, can be life-changing. Again, how does transformation happen? Not through thinking about it, and not through our existing filters. No one has ever transformed because someone else told them what they needed to fix – it has to be a process of self-discovery. We transform through experience.

Near the end of the first day of your retreat, give your participants an experience that allows them to see for themselves the patterns that have been getting in the way of their goals. Throughout your retreat give them opportunities to have new experiences that will define them going forward, knowing in their bones that though their old rules for doing life might have worked in the past, they are no longer serving them.

Ideally their new experience happens in the retreat. I've facilitated this in many different ways over the years, from having participants present in front of the room while embodying their new truth, to giving them a specific experience of asking and receiving such as asking someone in the room for something they need. Sometimes their new experience is enrolling in your HLP, giving themselves a container of support to take them to the next level with their goals. Often their new experience occurs spontaneously during impromptu coaching in front of the room.

In one retreat in Baltimore, we worked on money and owning your value. Baltimore had recently experienced riots in the downtown area and the energy was, well, a bit funky. Remember the woman I mentioned in chapter 5 who only brought twenty dollars spending money to the retreat? She was definitely in the market for a money breakthrough. She'd traveled a long distance with very little cash in her pocket, faithful that the breakthrough would help turn her money situation around.

The panhandlers on the streets of Baltimore were most certainly richer than she was, as a typical street performer in a touristy area averages $5,000 a month! And she was getting poorer by the day because she hadn't learned a skill that the panhandlers already had – the skill of asking.

As the participants held space for her breakthrough, I got her to acknowledge what it was costing her to go through life pretending to have it all sorted while underneath she was concerned about how she was going to survive the following week. She saw all the ways this pattern cost her. She discerned where in her life she'd invented the pattern of looking perfect on the outside and the associated belief that she shouldn't ask for anything, especially money. It explained why she'd been getting by with small amounts that had been donated for her services or fell into her lap while offering her skills. But she knew she had nice dreams and had a bigger mission to fund. She made the decision that she was no longer willing to live that way.

I then gave her the opportunity to give herself a new experience. I suggested that she seize the day, then and there, and ask someone for something (preferably money). Silence fell over the room as we waited to see what she was going to do. And we waited. And we waited. I pointed out that by choosing to ask for money in that moment she would break a lifetime pattern, and that it made total sense that she was terrified, as her subconscious mind had carefully crafted her "perfect" persona to keep her safe. This action would be totally outside her comfort zone, and to her subconscious it would feel like death. Her subconscious would need to invent a whole new way of being if she could do this and live, and that was why it felt like an impossible task.

We waited. The clock was eating into our lunch break and stomachs were growling, yet we waited. Everyone in the room could feel the power of the impending transformation.

People began to shift in their seats, glance at their cell phones for the time, and stare longingly at the coffee station, both cheering for her and feeling the ridiculousness of the situation. And there she sat, her face twisted with the obvious contemplation. Her ego fought for survival as she clung to her old belief about who she was. She was obviously debating the pros and cons of allowing herself to change.

Then she stood up shakily and walked over to another attendee and asked for her Kind Bar. Phew, she had broken the seal. But she knew she'd played it safe. I said, "Again. Ask again."

Then she asked the person sitting to her right for a dollar. "Again," I said.

She asked a woman across the room for twenty dollars, and received it. She was pushing her luck. Her next request went down to five dollars, but the person she asked had no cash. Then she did the unthinkable! One of the participants had just won a crisp hundred-dollar bill from me in a game we'd played. She'd been very excited, and she'd shared that she'd always been the one to give others money, time, and support, and she was never the one to receive. Everyone in the room knew that this hundo was sitting safely in her pocket as she sat in her seat at the far end of the room. The woman who was afraid to ask stood up and walked to this woman. The room was totally silent. She said, "Donna, may I have your hundred dollars?"

Wow! One experience quickly became two, because Donna now had a choice to make. Would she stay in her old pattern of giving to others or would she keep it and enjoy her winnings? "No, but thank you for asking," came the response.

The room held its breath. Would she ask again or allow this temporary defeat to stop her? We waited. Then she asked another participant for twenty dollars, and received it, then another. Strangely, she hadn't yet asked me, so I inquired about that. Something about authority. Ah-ha. Another opportunity to know that she had the right to ask anybody for anything. She asked me next.

When it started to feel fun and light, we knew a new possibility had been formed for her as someone who asks, receives, and even though rejected, can still survive and thrive.

Finally we could go to lunch! The whole room was shifted by the energy of what was now possible through the power of experience.

This was an unplanned lesson that made a huge impact on every single participant in that retreat. Yet it was absolutely consistent with the intention I'd held for the group, which was for them to know their value and break through whatever was stopping them from making great money in their businesses. I'd intentionally created a game that would allow them to see where they stopped themselves from this result, and then I seized the opportunity to demonstrate it in a very real way that impacted each of them.

Think not just in terms of teaching lessons, but also in terms of creating experiences. Here are a few quick tips:

- Experiences are nothing more than creating opportunities for someone to internalize patterns or ways of being.

- Experiences involve becoming present to "what is so." If you're afraid to acknowledge something, your participants won't feel safe to face it either. You must always be doing your own work to be able to lead them.

- Experiences do not have to take a long time – they can happen in an instant.

- A client can have a new experience you'll never even know about. Make them aware of the power of giving themselves a new experience.

- Experiences that force people out of their comfort zones can be super powerful even if you aren't sure what they will get! (Such as ziplining, improv comedy, and more!)

- How you frame an exercise has a huge impact on the depth to which participants experience it. Don't just go through the motions; make every step important. It's the way you present the exercise that allows your participants to recognize the transformation in the experience.

- Remember that how participants are *being* in an exercise is a reflection of how they are being in other areas of their lives. Some want to avoid this truth. Hold firm to making the opportunity available for them to see it!

EXERCISE:

Your Intentions for Your Retreat

Take a moment to set the three intentions for your upcoming RR: the intention for your participants, one for your business, and one for you! This will help you get excited about marketing and filling that retreat with an abundance of STAR clients!

Speaking of STAR clients, in the next chapter we're going to explore the fun of understanding how you will serve your STARs by inviting them to work with you in your HLP after your retreat. This is my favorite part of your retreat agenda because it's where you generate your six-figure payday!

Chapter 11

Serving your STARs – The Six-Figure Payday

I was in Keystone, Colorado. The air was crisp and the day was bubbling with potential. I was hosting my latest retreat, which I was calling Retreat and Grow Rich LIVE, the predecessor to the "Essentials" retreat I run today. We were heading into the third day of our four-and-a-half-day experience, and I had no plan. The evening before we'd gone out for one of the most fun excursions I'd ever had on a retreat, the "Chuckwagon."

Since I was teaching them about retreats and what goes into planning the logistics of an excursion on a retreat, I wanted to give them the experience of an excursion. We walked to our departure point, hopped in a horse-drawn wagon, and were driven through some of the most beautiful scenery around to some buildings at the edge of a field. There were games like hula-hoop, a delicious meal by a campfire, and songs. It was loads of fun and a clear bonding experience.

The next morning I reflected, as I always do throughout my retreats, on who was in the retreat, what they needed most, and how I could serve them. This group was truly unique. Because this was a longer retreat, I'd charged a higher price for it, though I allowed my high-level clients to attend for free. There were three participants who were not current clients and five who were already high-level clients. I always like to have a couple of current clients attend because they can be the best advocates for working with me, but this group felt out of proportion – the clients outnumbered the prospects. I always make an offer at my retreats – first because that's how I make money! – but second because I know my attendees want to make sustainable changes in their lives, and offering a container of support really serves them. But most of this group already had a container with me!

So I wasn't sure what to do. I had noticed that they were asking *a lot* of questions. My participants usually ask questions, but this group in particular had questions in abundance! Many were specifically about how I coach in front of a room. They wanted to know how to "call someone on their shit," the phrase we affectionately use in coaching. They wanted to know how to decide when an exercise will work and when it won't. They wanted to know how I intuitively decide when to change course from what I had planned. And the questions kept coming. I knew this group was telling me something (remember my "EARN while you LEARN" mantra from chapter 8?), and I decided to tune in and find the lesson.

Since they had really bonded as a group the night before, on day three they started building on each other's questions even more than usual. They wanted to go deep. I could feel that they could really see themselves leading retreats, had bought in to the idea, and were nervous about whether they could create a great retreat. They wanted to be prepared for everything!

That evening my wife, Kimmi, and I sat down over a bottle of champagne to discuss how we could serve them. We had just sold our house and our realtor had given us a lovely bottle of bubbly to say congrats. We'd packed up all our things and sent them to storage in the city of our future home, and we were going to be on the road for two months! I needed this retreat to be profitable, and I wasn't sure I had an offering that suited my attendees' needs. It was clear that this group was after something very specific. Kimmi is also super intuitive, so together we felt confident we could come up with a plan.

We'd been on the road a lot in those months, and having seen so many people struggling to make a living, I'd been reflecting on why I was successful. I thought about a program I'd taken that had been offered in a room just like this one. The program included training for speaking in front of a room and an opportunity to do so. The fact that I felt I had no option but to get on stage and speak because I'd invested so much in the training really helped me recognize how much I'd been hiding. The experience of that speaking program transformed me in ways that I couldn't have predicted. I'd been teaching my RAGR curriculum for a little over a year while still offering my general business coaching, and now I was reflecting on how to help people move past their fears in more effective ways.

Champagne in hand, I began to talk with Kimmi about why my coaching was effective enough that these clients wanted to learn more. We talked about where we wanted to go in our lives in the coming months and what we could deliver that would really make a difference. We began to craft a new program, the Retreat Leaders Launchpad. It would include more in-depth training in how to coach in front of a room, detailed training in how to design and make an offer in front of a room, personal work on alignment, coaching practice, and feedback on coaching skills. We also envisioned a live retreat in which I would work with clients to develop and host a one-day retreat, giving them the opportunity to actually *do it*. We bundled in professional photography, which is a perk of being married to a brilliant photog!

We knew this program would meet the needs of the people in the current retreat, and we were both excited and nervous about sharing it! Could we do this? Would this serve our clients? What were we creating here at midnight in the midst of a champagne celebration? Oh my!

I've learned over the years that if an offer doesn't make me excited and just a bit nervous because it's so on the edge of creation, it's not going to go nearly as well as the ones that create butterflies in my stomach. I trashed the offer I knew wouldn't serve this specific group, and took a deep breath.

On day four I began by painting a picture of the difference my attendees were going to make through hosting their retreats. I talked about how challenging it can be when you are in the "hallway" – when you've closed the door to playing it safe but you haven't yet walked through the new door of your leadership; when you're wondering what it will be like to actually break through into unknown territory. I knew they had all the questions I had when I first started my business: "Will I be good at it?" "Will it work out?" "Are there things I don't know – that I don't even know I don't know?"

I shared my own experience in that same hallway. I told them about the time I gave my first talk in a practice setting in front of coaches who were there to give me feedback. I told them about having worn essentially all black and ending up in front of a black curtain, disappearing into the background. I told them how my voice shook, and that even though I'd spent ages on my content, who I was being was so painfully frightened that no one could listen to what I was saying because I didn't own it. I told them that had I not committed to that process, I would have likely stayed where I was, thinking about getting in front of people but never doing it.

Then I shared some details about what type of person is truly ready to catapult themselves and their business through the power of live retreats (which described nearly everyone in the room). I shared the reality that many entrepreneurs think about doing this, but never do; or they go for it, and wonder why it didn't work out for them. It was because they weren't able to see what was getting in the way, just as I couldn't see that I was blending into the black curtain in my own life.

Then I presented them with the opportunity to join the Retreat Leaders Launchpad. It would be a significant investment [for them and for me!], and was designed to transform them in a way that would pay dividends well into the future. Kimmi handed out the order forms. Six people filled them out and turned them in with deposits within the hour. While it took following up with them to sort out the details and confirm the fit (I didn't want anyone in the program who was not a match), we netted five people for a more-than-six-figure commitment of revenue for my company.

This was an unusual scenario. Ideally you want to know what you will offer on the back end when you begin a retreat. But I discovered that what I had to offer wouldn't serve the group, and I knew and believed deep down that life always works out in our favor – it's our job to pay attention to the signals.

By being open to what was happening in the room, not only did we create a six-figure payday, but the new program allowed me to discover what, specifically, my clients needed to know to jump full-on into their retreat-based businesses. This program now shapes everything I do! I now have a few clients who have developed the skill of trusting that Spirit has put the right people in the room with them, and have learned that they can remain open to how they position their HLP and tweak the details on the fly. That level of confidence in what you offer and how to connect with your clients is an irreplaceable business skill that grows with you.

You have to start somewhere, so let's make a plan for offering your HLP during your RICH Retreat, shall we?

You Can Create a Six-Figure Payday

If you've been in business and working with clients individually or in groups for some time, your main goal for retreats may be to increase your revenue, serve higher-level clients, or serve at a deeper level. If this is the case, you're perfectly poised to create a six-figure payday from your first retreat!

If you're new or newer to business and you're just getting comfortable with your message and the transformation you offer, you're not likely to have a six-figure retreat right out of the gate, and that's perfectly okay. You'll earn while you learn and grow your skills as a guide for your clients, and as you do you'll deliver more and more value.

There are lots of ways for money to come to you through retreats. You can host a high-end retreat with five or six people and charge $20,000+. This is uncommon and requires extreme clarity about the outcome and the value. But this type of retreat brings your payday in *before* the date of your retreat. I call this a "destination transformation retreat," and it's not the focus of this book. However, I do want you to know that it is completely possible. It requires a bit more planning, as the location is a large part of the draw and is usually somewhere exotic.

Most of you will host a small retreat to help generate your six figures in client contracts, so the money will come in during the six-, nine-, or twelve-month time period after the retreat. Your attendees will sign up for a container of support in the form of your HLP. Depending on how you designed your HLP in chapter 7, you will offer options to pay for it in monthly payments over the course of the program or to pay in full and save (I generally discount 10 percent for payment in full). The payment plan creates recurring revenue on your books for a committed time period and can really support you in creating a sense of freedom as you grow.

When my offer is truly aligned with my heart and with the content and experience of the live retreat, usually half of my retreat attendees want to continue to work with me in a higher-level program.

Let's say you have twelve people in your retreat. You can estimate that six will be future clients. You'd need to offer an HLP that is roughly $17,000 to generate six figures from your retreat. That's $1,400 monthly for a twelve-month program. If this seems out of the realm of possibility, go back to chapter 5 about offering and receiving. That said, it's totally okay if you want to work your way up to this level.

If your goal is to host larger retreats and enroll more clients in your programs, it might be more appropriate to offer a lower-priced HLP (remember the Desire-Based Pricing!). I usually advise clients to start with an HLP priced at approximately $1,000/month. With the right positioning, program design, and understanding of your value, anyone can achieve this. (And this is where I started.) It can be a $6,000 six-month program or a $12,000 twelve-month program.

Let's say your program is twelve months at $12,000. You would need nine clients to cross the six-figure line for the year. If you host two ten-person retreats, and half of your participants work with you further, you will have a six-figure income. Double your number of RRs OR double the investment in your HLP, and your multiple-six-figure business is just a few steps away.

This is where the work gets exciting! I've given you everything about my retreat business model and the exercises to help you think through its structure. Now I will share specifically how to craft the offer segment of your retreat. Yet I know some of you, likely many, might have trouble putting the pieces together because you still haven't embraced your value as a teacher and leader.

When I meet someone and learn a little bit about their goals and vision and the difference they want to make, I can easily envision their business model in front of me. I can see the value of their work, the rough structure of their HLP, and how they would offer it in full integrity to the right audience. Please know as you move through this chapter that if you are uncertain about how to craft your offer, you are not alone. This is exactly why I've designed programs and live experiences to not only put my expert eye on your business, but also help you know your value for yourself, deep down in your bones.

Serving Your STARs

As you're developing the offer for your HLP throughout this chapter, keep in mind that while we're talking about creating a six-figure payday, we are always coming from a place of service. You've carefully designed an offering with features that guide your clients from the pain at their bus stop to the benefits at their destination. As a result of the work in your HLP, your clients' lives will never be the same. This level of work with you is not for everyone. Some people will take your bus part way, get a quick immersion in your castle, and move on. This is completely okay. But your STAR clients – the ones who need you most – will gladly stay on your bus.

Offer Positioning 101 – Identifying Their Hallway

When my life was falling apart – when my stepdad had just died and I was preparing for the final stages of my divorce – I found myself in a therapist's office. I wasn't expecting much to happen inside those four stark walls in the office complex next to Chick-fil-A, but I didn't know what else to do. I needed someone to talk to. I needed support. Much to my surprise, my therapist gave me the keys to the kingdom in one short phrase. She said, "When one door opens, another door closes, but the hallways sure are a bitch."

I laughed a sad, knowing laugh. Then I let it really sink in. She was absolutely right. And I began to see that it wasn't that my world was falling apart and I had no place to call home; I was simply in a hallway. Granted, I didn't close the doors of my own accord, yet here I was in a place where the possibilities were endless if I could just find my way through the next open door.

I began to actually visualize myself in a hallway. I could see the new door some distance away. I knew it was my door – it had a flashing neon sign with my name on it. And I could see and feel that I had everything I needed to get through that door – I could feel the wind of Spirit at my back propelling me in that direction.

Yet I wasn't moving. I was frozen. I looked around and saw that there were all kinds of open doors. I had left doors open to potential careers I might want to explore as back-up plans in following what Spirit wanted for me. Some doors were wide open, such as "people pleasing," "waiting for the permission of others," and more. I could see that I needed to close some of these in order to let myself move into my doorway. And I needed guidance in the hallway, because I was clearly terrified to close some of those familiar doors. What if I picked the wrong ones to close? More important, there were doors I'd left open that I hadn't even noticed were there. I would have never seen them without help. Yes indeed, the hallway was a total bitch.

Your client is in the hallway. They might not realize it, but they are. If you've done a great job designing your retreat, you've helped them firmly close one door and they are right smack dab in the midst of a transformation. The key to positioning your HLP offer is in understanding the hallway they are in. What pain are they no longer willing to tolerate, and what is the desire that is pulling them forward through that door to freedom? The more insightfully you can paint a picture of this hallway, the more easily you will be able to help them see your ability to guide them through it.

One Offer, Multiple Hallways

There are multiple hallways where your STAR clients could be stranded when they come to you. While you've defined the qualities and personalities of your STAR clients, they may be in different stages of growth, or you might find there are different specific triggers in their lives that cause them to want to change.

For example, I work with a client who supports women who are unhappy in their marriages. She helps them take responsibility for what they have been bringing to the relationship, get really clear about what they want, and assess whether they can get that from their current partner. Then she helps them navigate the change by either being different in their marriage or taking the steps to leave. The personality of her STAR client is the overachiever, good girl, people-pleaser who may have chosen her marriage because it looked good on paper, but never really connected heart to heart. She's focused on being a star in her career, or an amazing mom to her kids, or both, rather than creating connection with her partner. Based on this understanding, we can begin to get a picture of where this person is. What are some doors that might close for her and force her into the hallway of taking a look at her marriage in a new way?

- Her kids leave for college and she now realizes how lonely her marriage is.
- She loses her job or it no longer fulfills her.
- Her partner says he or she is not happy.
- A new person at work starts flirting with her and it awakens a part of her that's been shut down for years.
- One partner cheats.
- She and her partner finally get to the dream house or financial status they longed for and realize it's empty.
- A parent dies, perhaps the one she was trying to please by marrying her partner.
- She or her partner gets sick, causing them to rely on one another more heavily and recognize their issues.
- They relocate for a job, no longer have the same friends or support system, and relying on one another no longer comes naturally.

There are a variety of things that could happen to wake this person up. As you brainstormed with your clients you would start to see that these events fit into a few categories:

- The loss of the thing that was filling them up or at least serving as a band-aid

- An external person or situation that wakes them up to what is missing in their intimate life
- Something that forces the couple to spend more time together

The insight about what led them into the hallway is slightly different for each of these scenarios. This is why understanding the intricacies of these triggers is important.

As you lead your retreat, tune in to who is in your room. What is really going on with them that has brought them here? There are generally patterns and trends in each specific retreat. I think of this as "energetic pull" – the people who were drawn to a particular retreat at a particular date and location were drawn there by a similar energy, and they are surprised and thrilled to find others there with similar stories and pain points. If you spend some time understanding the nature of their potential hallways, you'll be much better prepared to tailor your offer to the room on the fly.

As another example, those who find their way to my RAGR program tend to be in one of three places/hallways:

1) Frustration that they are struggling to make sales one-to-one
2) So busy with one-on-one clients that they aren't marketing or growing
3) Bored with selling information, and wanting to make a bigger difference

Wherever these clients find themselves, they are either going to close the door to that pattern willingly as they join my program, or the old way stops working, forcing them to make a change. Here's an excerpt from the beginning of my sales page that highlights these issues:

You are scrambling to offer 1-on-1 strategy sessions to fill your private programs, and you're tired of running into price resistance, especially because you know that you should be charging more!

*Or perhaps you are so **busy delivering your services 1-to-1 that you don't even have time to market**, and you've capped out your earning potential. It's fine for now, but you can't live like this forever.*

*Maybe you've got a business that's working — you're selling information and people are buying it — but **you're ready to take your impact to the next level**. You want to give your clients lasting transformation.*

See how I've used these hallways to nail down my sales copy? Since I know these are the reasons people are drawn to creating retreats with me, I can keep an eye out for the trends in any particular room and use my knowledge to tailor my offer so they can hear it and take positive action.

Reading the Room

This section is about structuring the specific flow of your offer in your room — how you actually talk about the HLP you give your attendees the opportunity to purchase. We covered *what* you are selling when you designed your HLP. This is about *how* you sell it.

There are many pathways for selling the same program. For one person, spending time in your castle brings changes to their health, relationships, and sense of personal freedom. For another it brings them more money and a sense of power. Same program, loads of different benefits. Take time to tune in to the nuances of each different group of people.

To be clear, this is not about tailoring your program for every need. That would have you running around in a land of crazy customization. It's about adapting how you talk about the program based on the real needs of those in your room. Your container is solid and it will get them the desired result. The way you present your offer should allow them to create their own personal intention for the outcome they will achieve by working with you. ***Their clear intention, based on their personal truth, is a huge part of why the container will work for them***. You are not setting the outcome, they are.

So how do you read your room? By simply paying attention. Below are four specific tools I use to focus my attention. These are gold for the intuitive business owner.

1) **Hear the Words**. This is more of an intention than a tool. Set the intention to not only hear but pay attention to the words your participants use. Does the same word or phrase keep coming up in conversation? For example, I remember clients saying that they felt they were "flip-flopping" and "ping-ponging" and using the word *flipping* to describe their inner world. This made for a great theme to describe the hallway in my offer. "It's time to stop the flip-flop and step into alignment" became the way I positioned my offer. You might hear attendees talking about wanting a "beach house," wanting to feel more of a sense of "order" in their lives, or wanting to experience "self-expression." These make great ways to position your offer. Set the intention that you will notice and remember the words that keep repeating in the room.

2) **The Daily Debrief**. Prepare in advance for your daily debrief by printing two or three copies of your roster with plenty of space to write after each name. I simply write each person's name on a piece of paper. At the end of each day, and even during lunch breaks depending on your time frame, spend about three minutes mentally scanning and tuning in to each person in the room, one at a time. Ask yourself, *At what stage is this person in their transformation, and what do they REALLY need?* Think beyond the surface need to the *truth* of what's really going on with them, and you will start to see the themes of the conversations you want to bring forward in the room. You'll not only gain insight that will guide you to dig deep with your participants, but you'll have a clear sense of how to position the offer.

3) **Feel Your Own Body**. It took me some time myself to develop this tool. I am intuitive and empathic, so I often feel what other people are feeling. I didn't know this at first or understand that this was even a thing. I can see now, looking back at my life, that this characteristic is probably a very big reason that I tuned my body out at an early age, rapidly gaining weight as a young girl, and became unable to describe to a doctor where my pain was. As I grew my own consciousness and identified with my body, I randomly experienced odd physical symptoms, which I first noticed during coaching calls. I'd get on the phone with someone and suddenly feel a strange physical pang in my chest, or get queasy. I didn't understand what was happening, so I started to ask clients how they were feeling physically in that moment. They would invariably describe the symptom I had picked up on. Then I began to notice that in retreats I could physically feel the collective energy in the room – upset stomachs, trouble sleeping, etc. If you've ever had this experience you are likely an empath – one who picks up what others are experiencing as if it were their own. I've learned how to listen to my body, receive its message, acknowledge the physical symptom, and let it go. This might not be a tool for everyone, but I want you to be aware of how this phenomenon works in case it shows up for you.

4) **Ask Your Team**. I always recommend having a team member in the back of the room who understands the principles you teach. Part of their job is to help you read the room. Ask them to make mental notes or write down things that seem unusual about participants when they register. Do they take issue with signing the confidentiality and release agreement? Do they show up late or frazzled? Do they have concerns or complaints when they arrive? Have your team member keep an eye on the interactions and body language in the room

during sessions and breaks. They will see things that you can't. Ask them for input as you develop your offer. What are the themes they are seeing? Do they jive with the ones you notice? Involving your team not only gives you great insight, but encourages your team to also buy in to the offer in a way that serves the energy of the room.

The HEART Offer Formula

To craft an offer I use the HEART offer formula. This framework helps you think through what you want to share with your participants, and can be used to write a sales page or registration page for your retreat and in almost any other context in which an offer is being made. It's a framework, so adapt it to your business, approach, and personality.

I mentioned earlier a quote from Blair Enns, whose book *The Win Without Pitching Manifesto* defines the job of a salesperson in a way that I love. He says that your role in making your offer is similar to your role in a sales conversation – **to have your prospect form the intent to solve their problem.**

As you craft your offer, don't ask yourself *How do I get them to buy from me?* First of all, that's gross. You are in business to be of service. Your job is to frame your client's problem so well that they can't help but see it, then let them know that there is a solution. You can even provide the exact steps to the solution. If you're doing a Castle-Tour retreat, you've likely been spending the last two days giving them the exact steps anyway, so by now they know that what they desire is actually possible.

Your offer should help them embrace where they are now, where they want to be, and what it actually takes to close the gap between the two. This helps them make the decision to close the gap by accepting your offer. Then you simply share the structure you've developed to guide and support them on that journey and make it easy, fast, and fun. Because you're the one who helped them form their intent, you get them better than anyone. And because your offer is in front of them *now*, in the moment they've decided to make a change, they are likely to choose your offer as their means of transformation.

Not everyone will want or need your HLP. Some will decide they don't actually want to make a change, and they are not your people (this usually shakes out to about 20 percent). Some will want to make the change and feel confident they can do it on their own with their current resources (another 20 percent). If they have formed the intent to solve their problem, you have done your job. If you've framed your offer up nicely, some will be 100 percent clear that they want your offer instantly (20 percent). The remaining 40 percent will need to sleep on it, check their bank balance, talk to a spouse, or are still afraid to move forward – some truth-based part of them wants to work with you further but a competing belief prevents them from getting clarity. You can spend time with them either one-on-one, during breaks, or in the group during the remaining segments of the retreat to uncover those competing beliefs and help them make a positive decision.

So now that we're clear on intent, let's take a look at the H.E.A.R.T. formula:

> H = Hallway
> E = Experience
> A = Audience
> R = Reality
> T = Trust

These are the five components to think through for every offer you make. Let's dive in.

H – Hallway. Earlier in the chapter you developed a list of hallways your STAR client might be inhabiting as they transition from the pain to the destination. You now have a hypothesis as to what the hallway is; but remain open to adjusting your hypothesis as you get to know your attendees.

When you make your offer, the first thing you'll do is paint a super-clear picture of the hallway. In an ideal world your teaching segment right before your offer relates directly to the hallway and helps build momentum to your offer.

You've paid attention to who is in your room, and you know what they are experiencing. When you choose the hallway to focus on, go all in and own that hallway in a big way. Describe what it's like in this hallway by sharing a story or teaching very directly about what this hallway feels like. For example, let's say most of the people in your room are there to build their businesses, and you discover that 90 percent of your attendees are actually still in jobs and haven't made full commitments to their businesses. You would want to talk about what this hallway is like in great detail. How do they feel in this hallway? What kinds of thoughts do they have? For example...

> You know you need to leave that job and forge your own path, but the thought of closing the door on that steady income is downright terrifying. What if it's the wrong decision and you fail? What if you have to go crawling back and start at the beginning? What if you start this business and you don't love it as much as you think you will?

Do you see how that would encourage participants to get present to what it's like in the hallway?

Sometimes the hallway isn't clear and you have to guess or even create it for them. If your guess is good, people will register. If you are a bit off, all is not lost, but it won't be quite as hot an offer.

At a recent retreat I hosted, the group was small and surprisingly quiet. They didn't connect as well as most groups and it was hard to get a read on their common struggles. As I thought about each of them individually and where they were in their journey, the biggest shift I felt they needed to make (whether they were aware of it or not) was to elevate themselves and their thinking about their value. They were thinking too small.

A few of them had been in business for quite a while, were still primarily selling individual sessions and small programs, and were not having an easy time seeing themselves as providers of bigger containers of support. The rest were working at their "regular jobs" and having a hard time seeing themselves let go of their safety nets and dive wholeheartedly into their new businesses. Participants in both groups had their own versions of being afraid of what people would think of them if they owned their value and elevated themselves to a higher level of thinking or a higher financial level.

I themed my offer "Elevate," and shared a story about being so afraid to elevate myself that I created all kinds of problems along the way to stop myself. I told them that my mother used to call me ungrateful, and because of this I was afraid to want or have more, still trying to prove to my mom that I was *not* ungrateful. I painted a picture of what it was like to be in that spot and what they would be missing if they didn't move through it to the other side where Spirit had a big mission for them.

"Elevate" really hit home for part of the group and encouraged them to make a change with me. Others committed to making change on their own, and I've been seeing them take action via social media.

Nobody in the room had said they wanted to elevate. I had to read between the lines and claim my hallway. You can paint the picture through your own story, a teaching, the story of a client, or a story you heard on the news, as long as it illustrates your point.

E – Experience. The second step is to let them know that you have experience in this hallway. If you told your story in the Hallway step, this can be as simple as saying, "Hey, I've been there. I, too, know what it's like to be _____ and to want to be _____, and because I've lived through it I can tell you with all certainty that this is possible for you, too."

If you used someone else's story or a teaching in the Hallway step, take some time to elaborate on your own story and experience in navigating the same hallway or in helping others navigate it successfully. The goal is to let them know that you are experienced in the same transition they are looking for. On a registration page, for example, this would be the short bio section. It says something to the effect of "I'm Darla LeDoux and I'm here taking a stand for you to make this change because I have been right where you are. I was once…".

When you share your experience, be present to the transformation you've had and inspired by what is possible for them. Your sharing cannot come from the head; it must come from the heart.

A – Audience. At this point in the offer, you very simply name your audience. You let them know that of all the people in the room, you are talking specifically to them. Ideally you are speaking to the heart of at least half the people in the room. Provide a short description of your person, from one sentence to a paragraph. For example, "If you are a _____ [fill in your STAR client description], you know exactly what I mean and you can see this for yourself as well." You've just shared your story of triumph, and you are letting them know that you are speaking directly to those who want that same triumph.

Here's another example: "If you are a heart-centered entrepreneur who knows deep down that operating from the heart is going to make a bigger difference in the world than living in your head, you know exactly what I mean and you can see this for yourself as well." Or, "If you are a powerful and passionate woman who has forgotten that you actually get to choose how you live your life and whether or not you want to stay married, you know exactly what I mean and you can see this for yourself as well."

Do you see how those who know you are talking to them will draw close and those who don't feel that connection will tune out? That is actually what you want to accomplish! You want to name your audience in a way that is polarizing.

Another approach you can use in your Audience step is a short visualization. It can go something like this:

> *Close your eyes. Now imagine yourself* _____ *[the destination]. If this thought lights you up; if you have butterflies in your stomach and you find yourself leaning forward; if* _____ *[a physical manifestation of the destination], I have something that is perfect for you.*

This takes the physical into account and brings their full body into the decision. If you go this route, be really clear about the physical sensations your clients would experience if they said yes. For example:

> "Close your eyes. Now imagine yourself *with absolutely no physical pain. You are strong and free and alive.* If this thought lights you up; if you have butterflies in your stomach and you find yourself leaning forward; if *you feel ten pounds lighter and ready to run,* I have something that is perfect for you."

Or,

> "Close your eyes. Now imagine yourself *having six months of recurring revenue that is contracted and committed.* Imagine yourself *knowing how much money you will make next month, and that you will make that money doing work you love with people you love on a schedule you love.* If this thought lights you up; if you have butterflies in your stomach and you find yourself leaning forward; if *you feel the tension in your shoulders relax and the weight of the world lift as you think about it,* I have something that is perfect for you."

R – Reality. The fourth step is a reality check. This where you shift from having participants form the intent to solve their problem, to having them think about the reality that the problem has been around a while and that it is not likely they will solve it alone. This is the pivot point into presenting your specific solution.

This part of the offer should be simple, short, and to the point. Here are some options for how to get them present to reality:

- "Most people who try to do this work by themselves get burned out and tired, and stop."
- "Most people who go it alone wind up missing the most important steps or getting stuck in their heads, and never finish because they can't see what they can't see about what they are missing."
- "Most people's home environments are not set up for them to succeed at this goal."
- "Statistics show that _____ [examples: 85 percent of businesses fail within the first five years; one in four people in our country is overweight; etc.]."
- "You need support, guidance, structure, and a mentor who has been there."

This is the wake-up-call moment that activates the idea that they need further help to achieve the transformation. You are saying, "You're going to need help because it's not very likely that you'll succeed without it."

This is the step that a lot of entrepreneurs need extra support with because they grapple with making this claim. Yet if you really think about it, this claim is true. Time and again we make resolutions to do things differently, yet our default tendencies are to go back to what is comfortable. Without a container to remind us that we are committed to long-term transformation, we are all susceptible to going backward.

If you don't believe that is true and that your service is necessary for most of the people in your room, you might want to look into a different line of work – better yet, reread chapters 3 and 4 about owning it!

T – Trust. In this step you present your program in a way that builds trust. Through the way you share it, let them know that:

1) You've thought it through and created a structured process.
2) You understand them and what they need.
3) You are going to follow through on what you promise.

Here is how you'll share your program in a way that builds trust: Introduce the program, overview the benefits, overview the features, confidently share the cost, present a call to action, and present an urgency bonus that gives them a reason to buy now. I go much deeper into this work in my RAGR program, but here's a short cheat sheet:

Introduce the Program

I've created a program that allows you to get the results you want without working alone in the dark to make it happen. I call it _____.

Benefits Overview

This program allows you to _____ so you can _____ and finally have _____.

Features Overview

Here's how it works: _____ [program name] _____ is an _____-week program designed to have you _____. It includes:

- Calls – step-by-step guidance through_____ (Value: $X)
- One-on-one or group sessions (Value: $X)
- Two-and-a-half days of _____ (Value: $X)

- A special bonus session on _____ (Value: $X)
(Ideally you give each of these features a really juicy name
that brings the benefit to life. For example, we call our group
sessions "*Own It, Baby* Community Power Hour" calls.)

Cost

The total value of this package is $_____. To do the work
with me privately would be $_____ and the investment if
you bought this exact program outside of this room would be
$_____. But because you've already invested time with me
today, I want to make you a special offer of $_____. Here
are the order forms.

Call to Action

You know this is right for you if you are feeling _____.
I like to work with people who are decision-makers, and this
is why I want you to make a decision before you leave this
retreat. Maybe you're nervous or you know you'll need to
redirect and reprioritize some money to make this happen, and
I get this – this is a great thing! Because it means you're going
to reprioritize your results. So as you take out your pen and
complete your order form, be ready, because I have one other
special thing for a lucky few of you.

Urgency

The first seven [or appropriate number] people who register will
get _____ [additional bonus]. I only have time for seven
[or appropriate number]. This will allow you to _____
[destination], and give me the chance to work with you further.
We are about to go on break now, so you have thirty minutes to
do what you need to do to make your decision. The first seven
people should hustle to the back table to turn in your order form
to our team. If you have questions to determine if this program
is right for you, I will be in the back of the room to help you
decide if it's the right fit. After the break we'll come back and
dive right into _____ [juicy content!].

EXERCISE:

Scripting Your Offer

Using the HEART formula, write out the general script for the offer you will make at your RR. You will be presenting to the room the opportunity to join you in your HLP that you designed back in chapter 7. This is a perfect next step for serving your STAR clients and getting them to their destinations after they leave the retreat.

Now that you have the foundation of your offer, we'll look at the other major skill to practice on your road to mastery – developing your automated Gateway Program and system for filling your retreats.

Chapter 12

Graduate Your Gateway + Your Automated Future

It was early 2010. I was networking three or four times a month and selling private coaching with me via individual conversations. I had the occasional speaking gig, which was awesome for positioning me as an expert. I didn't have any programs to offer. I was doing what so many new coaches do, offering three sessions a month at a flat monthly rate. Sometimes I would suggest that someone work with me for three months, but even then I didn't ensure they were *committed* for three months.

After weeks of playing with the numbers in my projected-revenue spreadsheet, I knew I needed to raise my rates. I was suddenly spending time around successful service providers who were charging WAY more than I, and I could see that I had the same level of skills and that I needed to charge what they were charging to create a business that worked. I needed to hire support and purchase technology, and I wanted a budget for that.

I was extremely nervous about raising my rates because many of the people I met locally did not seem to be in the habit of investing in themselves or their businesses. I was worried they wouldn't be able to afford higher prices, and I didn't want to leave them behind!

This was where I was in my thinking when I decided to host my first retreat. As I've mentioned, my first retreat, The Sweet Spot Business Intensive, was a big risk for me. I planned to fill it primarily by inviting my current and past clients. There was just one problem — there weren't very many of them! So I went to work bringing in more clients asap! Because my random month-at-a-time sales approach wouldn't help me get committed clients in the door before my retreat, and because I wanted to quickly have people say yes, I created a three-month group program that I could sell at a lower investment while I raised the rates on my private coaching and began to fill my retreat.

I increased the number of events I was attending to two per week, and put twelve women into this group program, which I called Destination Sweet Spot. I had a vague agenda for the curriculum and flow, but I committed to weekly group calls for twelve weeks, and decided about two days before each call what the curriculum would be for that week.

I must admit I was pretty nervous most of those weeks, as I had never done this before and didn't know how it would go. Before long I got into a groove and looked forward to these weekly calls. I excitedly invited my new students to my retreat, and most of them chose to attend!

Destination Sweet Spot was my first foray into a Gateway Program. Though I didn't know it at the time, I developed that small group for the exact same purpose that you will develop your Gateway — to create a group of clients who know, love, and trust you and are ready to attend your next retreat.

I eventually developed a structured curriculum for Destination Sweet Spot, and today my *fourth* Gateway Program is running — yes, I've had two others in between. I got a bit overzealous in my content development, but the system I used then is the same as the system I use today! (Please note that you don't want to have loads of different Gateway Programs, as each one requires attention and love to market, and multiple marketing messages will confuse your audience!)

Graduate Your Gateway

Give people a

What I did then that I still recommend now is I got into action, talked with people, got curious about their goals, and let them know I could help them. I brought in paying clients through the short-term program, gave them a taste of working with me, and then invited them to my retreat. You want to do that.

However, the reason I created the group program was because I was AFRAID people wouldn't want to pay to work with me privately, and I was also AFRAID to ask them directly to come to my retreat. I created extra work and stress for myself (which I've historically been quite good at!) by putting together the group while also developing my first retreat, and then some. A smarter solution for you is to create two offerings in the beginning:

1) A short-term program with either a three-month engagement of weekly, bi-weekly, or monthly sessions, or a one-day individual deep-dive retreat (often called a VIP Day)

2) Your RICH Retreat

When you're talking with a potential client, offer them the one-on-one program with a complimentary ticket to your retreat. That is your premium-priced offer. If money is an issue for them (reread chapter 5 first!), your RR is now the lower-priced *downsell* that you can offer them instead. This is a simpler version of what I did that can work well until it's time to "graduate your Gateway."

Your Gateway is a lower-priced program that you offer as a gateway to your other work – specifically as a gateway to your retreat.

My first attempt to launch that Decide Then Thrive online mastermind program didn't go well, and many people have the same experience marketing their first retreat. They get excited, write some marketing copy, send it to their list or post it to social media (the modern equivalent of distributing fliers), and expect people just to click and buy. And it doesn't happen. It's not because the retreat is not a great and inspired idea; it's just that they don't have an understanding of what it actually takes to fill a retreat. You don't want just anyone to attend, you want the right people who are choosing to transform with you. This sets you up for success with your overall RAGR system.

It is rare that someone who doesn't know you at all will click on your retreat and register. The last thing we want to do is fly across the country to spend time with someone and arrive there only to find that they aren't very good at what they do! Registering for a retreat is a risk. You want potential participants to get to know you in order to mitigate that risk for them.

In the beginning people will likely get to know you through one-on-one conversations. Whether you are speaking to a group, networking and meeting people in person and speaking with them one-on-one, or teaching a teleclass or webinar in which you offer a complimentary one-on-one strategy session, personal attention is the key to finding your retreat participants. They get to know you and feel your energy, and you can make a contribution to their transformation even before they buy in. A well-executed, ALIGNED Selling conversation builds the "know, like, and trust" factor quickly. They will then buy either your retreat or your one-on-one-plus-retreat bundle.

Eventually you'll want to fill your retreats without this manual process of having individual conversations with people. Eventually you'll want to graduate your Gateway to a streamlined, effective, and automated representation of your work that you absolutely love. Your ideal Gateway gives buyers a taste of what it's like to work with you, and leaves them wanting more.

Just as your RR is a chance to connect at a deep level, your Gateway is the first step in that journey. It's less of a commitment for your client in time, energy, and price. It gives them a feel for your approach.

The Gateway for most of my clients is a virtual course, usually four to twelve weeks in duration. The most common format includes lessons released weekly and periodic live Q&A calls while they are working their way through the program and/or personal access via Facebook or another forum. The live calls, webcasts, or other access to you allows clients to experience working with you personally. They get excited about being in a room with you! Your Gateway can be live with everyone going through it together all at once, or it can be automated so participants can join and end at any time (a.k.a. "rolling"). As an example, you can find the marketing and structure for my eight-week Gateway at RetreatandGrowRich.com/course.

Develop and host your first retreat and start your first (even small) group of clients in your High-Level Program before developing your Gateway. You will LEARN a great deal from your first retreat and your first group of clients, which gives you the EXPERIENCE you need to develop the best Gateway possible. You'll also have a higher and more predictable monthly income, which frees you up to be creative. I developed a very targeted course, which became The Biz School for Aligned Entrepreneurs, after having worked with clients privately long enough to know exactly how I could best serve them. That program served as my Gateway for more than four years before I narrowed my focus further to work with retreat leaders.

Many coaches out there on the Internet teach their clients to develop a virtual course FIRST. If you've taken one of those programs and you already have a course developed, great! You can use the strategies below to adapt your course as your Gateway for your retreat. But I've seen many people develop courses that didn't hit home for their clients because they hadn't yet worked with enough of them. Have patience and think of your Gateway as your work of art that you will proudly sell for years to come! I wish I'd understood this and waited, as my Destination Sweet Spot was quite short-lived!

Let's Have a House Party! Or Maybe a Tour!

Just as your RR can either be a House Party or a Castle Tour, so can your Gateway! You can do a Castle Tour, giving people an overview of each room in your castle with some training and exercises from each. This book is a Castle Tour of the Retreat and Grow Rich Castle, as is my Gateway. You can also choose to go deep in one specific room, as in a House Party.

Here's a hot tip: Many people think they need to have completely DIFFERENT programs and curriculum for their Gateway and their RR, but they can be the same! *I recommend keeping your life simple and streamlined by having the same, similar, or overlapping content in your Gateway and your RR.*

Why would someone pay for the same thing twice? For the same reason I wrote this book encouraging you to integrate retreats into your business! Just because someone has learned the INFORMATION does not mean they have integrated it. They likely did not receive the TRANSFORMATION you ultimately want for them.

Though studies vary drastically on this topic, I've read that only 12 to 20 percent of online courses actually get completed. Since you're reading *Retreat and Grow Rich*, you yourself have possibly had trouble completing a virtual program. You might like having the knowledge and information at your fingertips, but until you actually implement the first step, you are probably only moderately interested in the next step. I'd venture to guess that courses with higher completion rates also have increased *accountability*. And there's no better accountability than a date in your calendar when you will get together with others doing the same work, LIVE, to integrate what you've learned and claim your transformation!

Think of your Gateway as that container for the foundational information for your RR and HLP. Make it as experiential as possible by providing exercises and Q&A. Think of your RR as where the magic happens and your clients actually integrate the new awareness via live implementation and experience.

Your Automated Future

Selling your Gateway can be literally, or practically, automatic. It is completely possible to fill your HLP with ideal clients without leaving your office or picking up the phone, or by only speaking or sharing in person a few times a year.

But remember, you won't sell it by posting a virtual flier that says "Buy Now." You need to cultivate your client base. Connect with potential clients, give them value, and begin to educate them for free before offering them your Gateway. I recommend selecting one strategic pathway for doing this. I do it via automated marketing that happens in Facebook Ads. It took me a while to develop effective Facebook marketing.

There are many options for educating your future clients for free before they work with you, which I call "Drawbridge marketing," and you will want to find your own style; but the purpose behind this free and valuable content is the same regardless. Here are the top two intentions for your Drawbridge:

1) **Your potential clients have learned or agreed with the primary belief of your STAR clients.** My Drawbridge ensures that they know why they want to incorporate transformational small retreats into their business model asap, that they agree that intimate retreats and transformation really matter, and that they want to lead them.

2) **They are present to the problems in their lives that your program helps them solve.** Ideally they have also formed the intent to solve that problem and have chosen to buy your program, but your job is to help them see why they need the solution you offer. My marketing shows clients the lifestyle and impact they can create by choosing retreats over more time-intensive or less effective ways to deliver their services.

Remember that the reason for having a Gateway is to sell via automated marketing as opposed to filling your RR through personal conversations. Because a potential client can take a course from the comfort of their home, it's a safe way to get to know you. They don't have to wrestle with date conflicts and travel expenses at the moment of initial purchase. You've just reduced the barriers to working with you.

When you host your RR you want your clients to be prepared to transform when they arrive; you don't want them to be spectators. In your Gateway they can be spectators. It creates enough safety for them to try on the idea of the transformation you offer. Those who are ready for it will take the next leap to integrating the lessons by attending live.

When your full system is set up, you will *only* market your RR to those who have experienced your Gateway. You'll have a prescreened audience from which to pull STAR clients!

Invite to Integrate

When you have all three programs established, you'll have a consistent marketing approach that fills your Gateway through any of a hundred options, such as speaking engagements, being interviewed, online ads for your Gateway, and asking others to interview you. At this point your biggest job is to help potential clients understand the benefits of joining you live to integrate what they've learned and claim their transformation. Once they've seen your Drawbridge marketing and engaged in your Gateway, this job is relatively easy!

For years I offered my live retreat to my Gateway participants when they were about two-thirds of their way through the Gateway. Over the years roughly 50 percent of my Gateway clients went on to attend a live retreat.

Over the past year I tested selling my Gateway and my RR as a bundle. On average 75 percent of all purchasers attended a live retreat, which I love! That means 75 percent of my virtual clients get live transformation!

In the coming year, however, I plan to separate the two programs again. My retreats consistently sell out. As of this writing I'm still committed to intimate experiences in these retreats, and I lead them personally. I'm limited by my time and the number of bundles I can sell, and I don't want to limit the reach of this work! The world needs a transformation, and you and others like you sharing this work will make that happen!

EXERCISE:

Develop Your Gateway

Establish somewhere to gather insights and information for your Gateway. It can be a notebook, a flip chart, a white board, a computer file, or a drawer filled with Post-it notes. Don't rush to fill this space, but set it up to track your ideas for your Gateway over the next six months of client work and retreats.

As you gather information about what your clients need most in the very first step with you, you can begin to sort your content and assess your process. Tune in to your intuition. Will your Gateway be a House Party or a Castle Tour? Can you use the exact same content you share in your RR or will you give them a bigger or a smaller picture of the work?

We are coming to the end of our journey. In the next chapter I share the top mistakes entrepreneurs make when it comes to leading retreats. I've made most of these mistakes, so have no fear. If you're not quite ready to dig in to the mistakes just yet, feel free to skip to chapter 14 to wrap up with me in Transformation Nation!

Chapter 13

The Top Ten Mistakes and How to Avoid Them

When I hosted my second retreat ever, which required my team and I to get on a plane to Denver, Colorado, I discovered how much I loved the city. Within two years I'd decided to move there. But when I flew in for the first time, I was nervous. I was hosting back-to-back retreats at the same venue. There was a fulfillment retreat for clients who had signed up for my six-month container of support (HLP) at my first retreat. This went beautifully and I absolutely loved it. *And* there was a connection retreat I'd sold for $497, and twelve new potential clients were enrolled. I gave myself a day in between for hiking with my team in the beautiful Flatirons near Boulder.

I did everything just as I had the first time. I had my 182 PowerPoint slides. I had my binders that included handouts of all the slides, just as I'd seen people do at the big events I'd attended. I shared the same story. I moved at the same pace. I made the same offer (at a slightly higher investment of $8,000). Everything unfolded exactly the same – except my results. Rather than having six new clients excited to join my program, I had one. Rather than contracting $48,000, I had earned just a fraction of that.

Even though I'd been earning what felt like great money at the time, I had invested in my own growth through hiring mentors, and in my business growth through marketing sponsorships, at such a pace that I did not have the money in the bank to pay for the retreats I'd just hosted. I was counting on at least four new clients to fund the next six months. I panicked.

I get that my financial planning might sound highly irresponsible, especially if you'd watched me diligently check availability on each of my credit cards and determine which ones I would use to cover the balance when I checked out of the venue. Before I share the outcome of this story, I need to tell you that I would not change that circumstance for anything. For you to create the business and life of your dreams, you will do things that others would consider irresponsible. Period. You won't grow your business without risk. I would not be sharing my success with you in this book had I not repeatedly pushed myself out of my comfort zone, especially in those early years. Had I not invested in mentors who saw the possibilities for me that I couldn't yet envision, I would not have stepped out of hiding and impacted thousands of people. Had I not incurred expenses beyond what I could pay by trading my hours for dollars, I would not have found the courage to charge appropriately for the outcomes I helped my clients achieve.

This faith-based approach only works if you have a high-integrity relationship with your word and value the exchange of money. I've learned that there are people in this world who will pay for something and still not value it. And there are people for whom it is okay to not honor their agreements. As long as you aren't either of these types of people, you can absolutely make some "irresponsible" decisions that will force you to grow.

When I started coaching, I thought I could create my coaching business with no upfront investment. I was wrong. I'd done loads of personal-growth training and coach training and I was smart and committed, yet there was a whole lot I didn't know. Because of the strength of the support I'd sought, I was able to pause and regroup there in my Denver hotel room. As I stared at those wobbly credit cards, I momentarily felt like everything I had envisioned was not working. But I was quickly able to put it into perspective. I'd done the work on myself and I knew I was not defined by my job title or the money I earned. I was able to set my ego aside and disassociate myself from the word *failure*.

I also understood energy. I believed wholeheartedly that we are all energetically connected and that everything is always unfolding for our greatest good. I also knew that I was always the source of the results in my life. I had proven this to myself 100 percent. If I got a certain result, it was because something in my thinking had created that result.

So I went to work on two things: 1) Holding firm in my knowledge that this result was perfect and there was just something I wasn't seeing yet, and 2) Pondering the source of my result. Why hadn't I converted more clients? What was really going on? As a result of holding firm in my faith, I concluded that if those six clients hadn't been in the room, they must be somewhere else! This is when I set an intention by praying to the Universe to show me where they were.

I crafted a series of communications to my email list, which was about 700 people at the time, sharing the excitement of my retreat and offering sessions in my program. In the next ten days I got two new clients from this effort. While I was doing that I received one personal referral and one other person reached out to me at LinkedIn about what I was doing, even though I had done no active marketing there. Then one of the women who had attended my retreat changed her mind and decided to join me. She went on to be my client for the next two years.

I share this story because I want you to know that I have made mistakes along the way. I have had moments that felt like death. They have also led to my greatest moments of rebirth or deeper understanding.

I did in fact get to the source of my result of gaining only one client from the room that day. In part it was certainly to be able to share with you this story of faith and confidence and what it really takes to run a business. But there was also a distinct mistake I had made, which you will find in the list below. I share these mistakes with the intention of helping you avoid them and, even more powerful, to help you recognize them when they happen so you can shift quickly into the faith of knowing that all is unfolding perfectly.

Mistake #1: Undercharging

This is the most common mistake across the board. Some entrepreneurs believe the stories we discussed in chapter 4 about money being scarce, people with money being greedy, etc., or they think that while everyone else is awesome and ready to receive, they are not there yet. Maybe after one more certification....

People don't value what they aren't invested in. Different people have different ways of viewing money and feel stretched at different price points. There is not one set price for all retreats and all providers, and you will make choices about how big you want your community of clients to be and what lifestyle aligns with you. Use the approaches I've shared in this book, including Desire-Based Pricing for your HLP (chapter 7) and break-even pricing for your RR (chapter 9). When someone's programs aren't selling, they can very quickly panic and drop the price when what they truly need to do is raise the price to get people's attention!

Mistake #2: Overcharging

You might find this surprising given mistake #1! You definitely want to price your HLP at a rate that makes you feel a bit stretched, but at which you can still envision receiving that money. If you feel out of alignment with your rate, people will feel that. (At my Retreat and Grow Rich Essentials LIVE retreat we do exercises about finding the right price point by uncovering your true desires, and you get to practice quoting rates, which helps tremendously!)

Where I most see people shoot themselves in the foot is in pricing their RR, whether they become afraid about it working as a client connection / marketing strategy that will make them money on the back end, or they feel that it won't look good if they charge too little. It's hard to lower the price once you put it out there, though raising the price is relatively easy as you gain traction. The last thing you want to do is create price resistance when you want to bring people into the room for your first retreat. I've offered retreats at all different price points, from $247 to $25,000, and here's what you need to know:

Don't overthink it. It doesn't really matter what you charge unless you are doing a major all-inclusive destination transformation retreat, for which you should be paid very well. Keep the big picture in mind. Not only are you allowing potential lifelong clients to get to know, like, and trust you, but you also get to earn while you learn. You'll have a built-in focus group from whom you will learn and grow. You'll deepen your understanding of yourself, your content, and your ideal and non-ideal tribe members. You'll create more insightful marketing and grow the long-term viability of your business. But you have to get the people in the room. (When I worked at Procter & Gamble we paid five figures to an agency to gather groups of our ideal clients in a room so we could ask them questions for an hour!)

Price your retreat so that you'll cover your expenses with just six people in the room. For most people this is between $500 and $1,000. Any additional attendees earn you extra cash, but the focus is on building long-term clients in your HLP.

Price your services high enough for clients to become truly invested. If you're wondering if $500 is high enough for them to feel invested, remember that anyone who is going to spend nights away from home, book a flight, find a dogsitter, etc., is going to be invested. Retreating is not convenient. It is a commitment. Trust that.

Mistake #3: Too Much Content

I recently had a retreat participant who had developed a very specific process for increasing your consciousness and therefore creating more success in your life and work. It was an eight-step process and had created profound results for him and the handful of people he'd worked with using this process. He'd offered a few workshops, loved his process, and felt the attendees had loved it, but he was left with no clients – they were happy with the workshops but they weren't converting.

When I uncovered what he'd been teaching, I saw that he had been putting two-and-a-half days' worth of work into a two-hour workshop. It was a classic case of too much content. His attendees could see the value of what they were getting, but they were not remotely able to integrate it in that period of time. And because it was a short, free workshop, they were not invested in the outcome.

As we began to work together on the two-and-a-half-day retreat content, he again defaulted to the fire-hose approach, addressing several areas of his clients' lives and multiple results. As we walked through the flow of his retreat together, he learned that by doing this he was showing how much his tool could do and how valuable this work was rather than focusing on integrating the process and leaving with one solid result.

What was great about this shift and insight for him was that the new design we came up with set the client up to want to work with him further over time to continue getting additional results. It also helped the client trust him as a guide who would not just share the steps but present them in a way that would truly serve them. This level of discipline is actually part of the service you offer!

Mistake #4: Having It All Together

It is inevitable that things will happen in your retreat that are not at all what you planned. You'll have someone in the room who is different than you imagined. The hotel will make a mistake and you'll have to improvise. You or a team member will make a mistake. Weather will interfere. (I have had tornadoes, hailstorms, and even a haboob (sandstorm) happen during retreats in various cities!) A mother will die. A car will slide off the road. You'll forget to pack your makeup. You name it, shit happens. If you are committed to having it all together, these things can break you. You want to show up with a plan to be human, real, and vulnerable. Doing this while still owning the room and instilling confidence is an art one develops over time.

One of the reasons people will come to know, like, and trust you is that you have let them really see *you* – not that you've presented them with a perfectly crafted version of you. That version can provide value, but it won't instill the trust they need to go on a transformational journey with you that will leave a lasting impact on their lives.

If something comes up that triggers or concerns you, find a way to move through it by telling the truth. "Let your panties show!" as they say. If you're not sure how, call your coach! I've handled everything from a nightmare venue in a post-riot city to a group that needed something totally different from what I planned to teach, a participant who clearly did not want to be there, and then some. I had to find ways to be transparent and move through these obstacles with grace. These were the moments that built trust above and beyond when everything went as planned. Trust the divine imperfection.

Mistake #5: Bringing Everyone with You

It is a human tendency, especially when you are a person of great integrity, to want to bring everyone with you; but not everyone in your retreat will get the same result. When you have the desire to look good and make everybody happy, you don't actually serve the room. If you focus on the perceived laggards and take too much time trying get them to understand, you will affect the positive energy in the room and annoy and bore your STAR clients who are right with you and wanting more. Teach to the STARs and trust that the others will get what they need for this stage of the journey. They might not pop or have their profound and lasting insight right there in the room – it might be years later that they find themselves in a scenario in which your teaching comes back to them and suddenly they get it. Let that be okay or you'll make yourself miserable. And keep in mind that someone might pop quietly in their seat and you'll never know it. Sometimes my best long-term clients didn't say much of anything at the retreat.

Mistake #6: Loose Logistics

I have a love-hate relationship with structure. I prefer keeping things loose. I like to flow where the energy takes me. I value a back-of-the-room support person who keeps me on time.

The specific instructions you give for logistics of an exercise can make or break your retreat. This is a small thing, and your attendees will forgive you if you haven't thought through everything for a particular exercise or if you try something that doesn't work. However, if the flow of your exercises is consistently poor, they will eventually give up and stop playing.

Let's say you conduct an exercise that involves working with a partner. There is a listening step and a responding step. You can give the full instructions first, then have them find their partner; or you can have them find their partner first, then provide the rest of the instructions. Think through beforehand which way works best and best fits your style. If you say, "In this exercise you'll work with a partner," as you go on to describe the exercise, they will likely have stopped listening because they are making hand gestures to potential partners across the room. If you say, "Listen to the complete instructions before you choose your partner," they will listen. And you can save everyone time by being very specific, such as saying, "The person with the shortest hair goes first." Being specific about these small details saves time and prevents confusion that detracts from transformation.

Mistake #7: Tight Schedule

This mistake often goes hand in hand with too much content. It's a constant battle for me because I always want to put one more thing in and offer a really full experience. Be sure you leave space in the schedule each day for "insights, ah-has, and questions," as I phrase it. These are some of the richest and juiciest moments, and you want to have time to coach people as necessary when they arise. Leave ample time in your schedule for Spirit to show up through one of your participants and reveal something that helps everyone. If everything is planned, there's no space for Spirit.

You also want to give your participants ample opportunity to connect through sharing and being vulnerable. This can also happen during long lunch breaks and organized dinner outings. Space and grace, Baby – magic words, especially for type-A entrepreneurs!

Mistake #8: Not Getting Comfortable with Money

While your retreat could be your springboard for your first big payday, don't wait for your retreat to get comfortable with talking about money. Before your retreat, have conversations with people in which you ask for money, share your rates, and talk about money in any way possible to become comfortable talking about things that make others uncomfortable. The more you can stretch your comfort-zone muscle in this way, the better. If you can get at least one client to commit to your HLP before your retreat, it will feel more real and you'll be more excited about adding more clients. So go out there and have those conversations!

Mistake #9: Not Being Supported

If you host an intimate retreat you might feel like you can do it yourself – it's not a big deal, there aren't a lot of supplies needed, and you can do it more simply and cheaply by yourself. But even if you have just two attendees, it's a mistake to forgo back-of-the-room support.

First, you won't command ownership of the room and demonstrate expertise if you are also the one schlepping your flip chart down the hall and sitting at the table handing out name badges. You are the CEO and sought-after expert (even if it is your first retreat), and you should treat yourself as such.

Second, when things come up like the room is too cold or an attendee steps out to take a phone call and doesn't come back for an extended period of time, you need someone who can handle these things. "Jana, can you check on Susie for me?" This not only helps Susie, but also lets everyone in the room know that you care about Susie, and therefore you care about them, without having to stop the flow to handle things.

Third, your support person has a view of the room and the attendees that you don't have. They see when someone shows up late and disheveled and whether they are rude or gracious when they register. They know who's nervous, who had something happen on the way to registration, who already knows each other, who's having distracting side conversations, and who might be a problem participant (a.k.a. "the gift"). Having someone who can give you a heads-up about such things is huge. And last, you need a safe person with whom to vent or process. You need that person to hear whatever you need to work through without creating any stories or judgments about it. If you are triggered, you need to clear your reaction quickly so you can move forward. That is part of their job. Train them how to do this! (I teach this training in my RAGR virtual course.) Providing leadership during the time leading up to the retreat enables your people to support you when you need it.

Mistake #10: Treating All Rooms the Same

This is the mistake I made in the story at the beginning of this chapter. In my second retreat I assumed I could just do the exact same thing I did in my first retreat without understanding the organic nature of a personal-growth business. One of my coaches often used the phrase "Rinse and repeat." Because I always loved to focus on developing something "right" so it would be perfect and aligned and never need to be touched again, I LOVED this idea. I longed for things to be on autopilot, never to be touched again. Let the money roll in without any effort and coast the rest of my life away. Ha!

"Rinse and repeat" is a nice idea, and the system I've shared in this book allows you to repurpose many things and to eventually sell your Gateway Program using automated technology. I've done this in my own business and it's wonderful. But I am under no illusion that I can simply forget that automated marketing and never revise or update it. We grow, society grows, and trends and energies change constantly. Your business is not a static entity. The sooner you embrace this, the happier you will be.

Breathe new life into your business on a regular basis for it to return life to you. Develop a profound awareness of your growth. While the baseline marketing for your retreat can remain the same (a single registration page can last for years without updates), the message you use to draw people in should change over time. You'll teach something fresh in your webinar, or share a different message on social media or in your live networking events, based on how you've personally grown and learned to see things with fresh eyes.

This is actually a great thing. You continue to deepen your expertise, and each group of people in your retreat is unique and interesting, causing your full engagement and the acquiring of new knowledge.

This is what I didn't understand in my second retreat. I wanted to be the same person and do the same things to create the same result. Only I wasn't the same. And neither were my clients.

There was one client in my first retreat who told me in passing that she wanted "little elves to run her business." I'd assumed she was kidding, and stepped over that statement. She was very difficult to work with because she had, in fact, not been kidding. She didn't want to do the work. From that experience I learned that I wanted to create a higher bar for who I let into my program. I only learned this upon deep reflection, and I used it to help me find balance in how I make offers.

I also grew so much in my own consciousness that I wasn't sure my retreat participants were ready to grow with me. My rinse-and-repeat mentor also taught me that my list of email subscribers is generally ninety days behind where I am in my growth. Because my second retreat was just a couple of months after my first, my list hadn't quite caught up with me, and therefore the people in the room weren't quite ready to be "my people" on that leg of the journey; I challenged them too much.

My third retreat was the first in which I broke six figures in contracted revenue. Because of the mistakes of my second retreat, I understood what I was doing a bit better. I put the right people in the room using the power of my intention, ditched the binder, cut my PowerPoint slides in half, and approached my offer with confidence. It was magical.

You can do this, too. You can learn from my mistakes or make your own, and as long as you hold firm in your faith in your mission – in the clarity of your why and the knowledge of your value – you absolutely cannot fail. All temporary setbacks are springboards for future breakthroughs, and the cycle of your growth will continue.

If this sounds hard – if you're wondering if it's all worth it – join me in my final chapter to remember why you are in the exact right place and time to let your SELF be seen.

EXERCISE:

Plan for Mistakes

Review the list of mistakes above. Which do you think you'd be most apt to make? Create a strategy now to head that off at the pass!

Congratulations on the work you've done to Retreat and Grow Rich! I am *very* excited about the work you're about to do in the world to connect us with one another and empower us to grow. Join me in the next chapter for a proper celebration of our future as a Transformation Nation!

Chapter 14

Transformation Nation

For almost thirty years, from the time I was four years old and discovered I had been gaining weight until my early thirties when I let myself transform it, I carefully analyzed everything I ate. During the last years of those thirty I analyzed the calories, fat, carbs, and protein in my food. But what I was really analyzing was whether what I was choosing to eat made me a "good person" or was a harsh reflection of a defect in my character. I was taught to analyze this way. "Are you sure you want to eat that?" was a common question I fielded at the dinner table, at snack time, and any time in between.

It was in a transformational live retreat that I became present to the impact of this habit – I was expending countless units of energy pre-thinking about what I would eat tomorrow and reflecting on my food intake and weight the day before. I regularly placed my hand on my stomach and *hated* what I felt. (My physical health and appearance were actually just fine, wavering between average and a few extra pounds.) This was conditioned thinking. During an exercise in which we were directed to look at areas of our lives that were not working, food is what I choose. When I got present to the day-to-day impact that this food baggage had on my level of power and presence, I was astounded.

I was done with it! I was able to pinpoint the creation of the belief that something was wrong with me in regard to food to a specific day when I was probably five years old. We were living in an apartment above my grandparents' garage. My mother was working as a bank teller and she was often gone during the day. I spent much of my time with my grandma, but some days a neighbor would watch me. That day my mother, running late for work, sent me next door to Mrs. Wilberg's house on my own for the few hours until Grandma came home. As she sent me out the door, she pinned *a sign* to the front of my shirt that read "Please do not feed me."

Apparently I'd come home sick after eating too much candy at the neighbor's before, and this was her solution. I didn't fully understand, but I was mortified. I knew there something wrong with me requiring this extreme measure. My relationship with food was never the same... not until the moment in that retreat when I chose to bring it forward to transform.

It took great courage, as I'd been carrying the energy of "Please do not feed me" for years. The expertly guided exercise, done with a partner who held a very safe space for me, allowed me to bring forward that experience, share it, reinterpret it, and release the stored energy around it... permanently. My relationship to food transformed forever in that moment. I actually began to forget about my meals, forget to pack a lunch for work, and sometimes forget to eat altogether. This, of course, introduced a new set of issues! But as you can imagine, for the first time I felt free! (I also stopped feeling my stomach and shaming my body for its existence, which has been transformational in other ways!)

This is the life-changing power of transformation and facing our personal truths.

Normalizing Transformation

At the time the transformation took place, I barely shared it with anyone. It didn't feel safe or socially acceptable to talk about this strange occurrence at age five that had created a pattern of pain for nearly thirty years. Who would I tell? What would they think?

Would it matter? Today there are almost exclusively people in my life I *would* tell and who would understand because they, too, are on their own transformational journeys. But it still takes courage to share things that I discover aren't fully working and to feel safe to change them without fear of being judged.

I shared this story with you to inspire you to lead! Imagine a world in which it is normal to become aware of patterns that keep us stuck, to talk about them, and to actually do something about them! A world in which complaining, pushing, causing conflict, and thinking like a victim dissipate, and empowerment takes hold. A world in which individuals understand and VALUE the expertise of soft-skills leaders – the R.I.C.H. (Right-brained, Intuitive, Connected, and Heart-Centered) leaders who are holding space for this transformation to occur.

Imagine kids growing up in a world in which every family has a budget for transformational experiences and looks forward to choosing how to use it! What if each human being understood how to identify when it's time to face a new level of truth about who they are being and how to shift it? What if my mom had known that my putting on weight was a symptom of a deeper hurt that I needed to address rather than a character defect that needed to be combatted by force?

I'm sure you realize this mindset would have a ripple effect beyond solving individual problems. It would fundamentally change the vibration of the planet, creating more freedom, peace, and joy all around. And it all starts with the truth, acceptance, and validation available in the transformational small retreat.

Relax, You Are Already RICH

Retreat Leader, you already have the skills to create this kind of transformation. You would not have picked up *Retreat and Grow Rich* if you didn't. Your RICH skills – your soft skills – have developed over a lifetime of experiences, both painful and inspiring, and they are yours to claim. The more you recognize and honor them, the faster they will develop and grow.

Many entrepreneurs make the mistake of dismissing their inner knowing and their fleeting intuitive hits and clinging to their logical minds, or worse, to the logic of other "experts." I've learned loads from experts. I do not diminish that. I brought you this book as an expert. And yet every move I've made in business that has TRULY created deep transformation – for me or others – has come from following my own carefully honed soft skills and putting them into action – sometimes white-knuckled with fear, though mostly in freedom and flow.

It is an inside job to own your Right-brained, Intuitive, Connected, and Heart-centered ideas and risk putting them out there. Yet the shift in perspective needed to see them and tune in to them is often best done with guidance and in community with a group of like-minded seekers on similar journeys. This is why retreat leaders like you love creating RICH retreats in community at my Retreat and Grow Rich Essentials LIVE retreats!

You already have what you need to be RICH, inside and out, yet it is totally normal to need support in owning it!

> To start that journey with my guidance, I've created an ideal next step for you at **RetreatandGrowRich.com/RICH**.

Be Rich in Money, Too

Throughout this book I shared the practical details of structuring and pricing your offerings, including a section on the mindset of receiving money. Having the money to support your desires is important in being the leader you are here to be in the world. Yet there's more.

I'm passionate about creating containers of support for your clients that truly transform, *and charging well for them*. Why? Because if *you*, the person who is passionate about creating change, don't

VALUE your work at the level of a project manager, engineer, attorney, or CEO, how will our value system as a society ever change? It is time to stop buying in to the idea that this woo-woo or soft-skills work is somehow less valuable than that of our logical, linear counterparts. It's up to each of us to both increase the VALUE of doing this work with excellence and pave the way for others to follow in our footsteps as we make the work of transformation mainstream.

So that the next generation doesn't have to choose between a "helping profession" and money — a choice I made that cost me many years in poor-fit careers and suppressing what I knew to be true... what do you say? Will you join me in this mission? A Transformation Nation is within our reach. The time is now. The world needs your genius.

Acknowledgments

After three attempts to write my first book, I am so happy that it was born in alignment with my passion for retreats.

I would have never discovered my passion or had the courage to see it through without the support of friends, colleagues, and mentors who have been a part of my journey.

As each twist of fate helped bring me here, I am in gratitude for it all and would like to acknowledge everyone, but I'll start here:

Thank you friends who gathered round my table in Cincinnati as I attempted to sort through what the heck I was doing, especially Mary Carmen Gasco-Buisson, Claudia Sandman, Shawnta Buckner, and Virginia Pankratz. Thank you for believing something was possible even when you likely thought my pursuit would end badly!

Thank you to my early mentors who had no idea they were leading me along my path, including Susie Mills, Marion Corbin-Mayer, Michelle Johnson, Michelle Conboy, Jose Garza, Joan Cutlip, Steve Farrell, Trish Harpring, Dave Fazio who told me to become an engineer, Kathy Zubich who cultivated my early love of "helping," and Debbie Finn who ignored my math skills and encouraged me to write.

Thank you to my mentors who taught me business and mindset and helped me to see more of who I am in ways that have shown their value time and time again: Valerie Young, Suzanne Evans, Mastin Kipp, Justin Livingston, Stephanie Tuss, Erin Melnick, and so many more. And of course, David Neagle. Thank you for setting me free, and of course for making me gay. <3

Thank you to my mother who has been my teacher in more ways than she can imagine. To my father who made me independent and resourceful. To my stepfather with whom I had a bond beyond this lifetime, and whose death helped to free me from my fear.

Thank you to my sister Valerie who is a strong, beautiful woman and an amazing mother, and my brother Wyatt whose journey has been inextricably linked with mine. I love you.

I am in gratitude for each and every "mastermind friend" I've made along my business journey. The late-night hotel-room conversations and "hotseat" love will never be forgotten. You know who you are.

Thank you to my book team, including the amazing Pat Verducci and Lynne Klippel. Wow – we did it! And Amy Derr and Jana Rezucha, and the awesome contractors I've hired, who have picked up the slack as I stepped away to write.

And a special thanks to Kristi Johnson and Stacey Adams for always being a phone call away, and giving me the gift of non-judgment and the space in which to grow.

Thank you to Carol and Clay Ward for your unquestioning support of me and my work. You inspire me!

And last, thank you Kimmi Ward for entering my life. Thank you for being my partner in adventure, my sounding board, my rock, my lover, and my best friend. For holding space while I pushed my own resistance to write this book, and the 82,000 other things I've written since the day we met. I know this isn't the book you would have liked me to write, but thanks for trusting me; and "The Hallways" are coming!

About the Author

Darla LeDoux is a business coach and leader of sold-out transformational retreats across the globe. In business since 2010 she's generated millions of dollars in revenue and supported hundreds of clients to align with their truth and maximize their profits. She believes that intimate retreats have the power to heal and transform beyond one-on-one work or information alone, and are precisely what's needed in the world today.

A "recovering engineer", Darla graduated with a BS in chemical engineering from the University of Minnesota and held senior roles in marketing and product development at Procter & Gamble. She resisted the call to the world of coaching and transformation for years until death and divorce helped her find her courage.

Stepping into her true purpose, Darla grew Aligned Entrepreneurs using a core strategy of hosting intimate retreats, her first in 2010. Four years later she recognized that her clients longed for the same ease and deep transformation in their businesses that the retreat approach provided, and Retreat and Grow Rich was born™. Now Aligned Entrepreneurs is on a mission to make coaches, consultants, and healers wealthy from their deepest work with the transformational power of retreats.

Darla envisions a world in which regularly scheduled transformational experiences are the norm, not the exception. *Retreat and Grow Rich* is her first book.

Additional Resources

Throughout this book I've offered resources that will help simplify your journey. I've summarized them here for your convenience.

Grab sample retreat agendas including a blank template to make your planning easier at **retreatandgrowrich.com/agendas**.

Download my article series on the Top 10 Ways to Up Your Captivation Factor, making you a natural in front of the room, at: **retreatandgrowrich.com/captivate**.

Read the whole book? I've crafted the perfect next step for you, updated with the latest tips and trends for RICH Retreat Leaders, at **retreatandgrowrich.com/RICH**.

If you love this book and you want to engage with me and my community of the world's best transformational retreat leaders more deeply, you'll want to check out:

> Our free Facebook group, "Aligned Entrepreneurs Tribe." I am in there regularly sharing and connecting.

> Our guided course, which includes access to me directly to answer your questions and guide your retreat and program development. It's the content of this book on steroids, complete with videos, worksheets, and office hours. You can register at **retreatandgrowrich.com/course**.

Meet me in person! If you're like me and you like to give yourself the experience of getting it done, check out the dates for our next LIVE retreat at **retreatandgrowrich.com/retreat**.